Dynamic Enterprise Architecture

How to Make It Work

Roel Wagter

Martin van den Berg

Joost Luijpers

Marlies van Steenbergen

WILEY

John Wiley & Sons, Inc.

Library of Congress Cataloging-in-Publication Data

Dynamic architecture : how to make enterprise architecture a success / Martin van
den Berg ... [et al.].
    p. cm.
  Translated from Dutch.
  Includes bibliographical references and index.
  ISBN 0-471-68272-1 (cloth)
  1. Strategic planning. 2. Organizational change. 3. Business enterprises—
Communication systems—Management. 4. Information technology—Management.
5. Industrial organization. I. Berg, Martin van den, 1955–
  HD30.28.D923 2005
  658.4'038—dc22

                      2004018702

Printed in the United States of America

10 9 8 7 6 5 4 3 2 1

CONTENTS

PREFACE

Since the publication of this book in the Netherlands in 2001, our approach to dynamic enterprise architecture has taken off. We were the first to address the everyday ups and downs that organizations face in enterprise architecture. Our initial audience—organizations that had some experience with enterprise architecture and those new to the concept—benefited from that first edition. Experienced organizations discovered why enterprise architecture had not yet brought them all the expected benefits. Novice organizations learned to not make the mistakes that others have without the experience. This edition promises the same: a better understanding of the processes involved in successfully employing architectural thinking and the tools to analyze a situation and identify the points of improvement.

How do you improve your business using information technology (IT)? This question has obsessed us. A few years ago, we started to turn our ideas into a model. Architecture is the *leitmotif* of all these ideas. We believe it is the main tool for the effective and efficient application of IT's potential. This basic idea constitutes the origin of DYA® (**DY**namic **A**rchitecture for modelling and development) as a conceptual and practical model.

Over a period of two years, DYA matured and was tested, elaborated, discussed, and communicated. This book is the end result of that process. This vision has been detailed in a conceptual and practical model that provides for the setup and professionalization of architectural processes in an organization.

Writing this book was a major challenge. The concept of architecture in the IT industry has many aspects. When you ask ten architects to define architecture, you will get ten different answers. Nevertheless, we engaged in discussions with other experts when writing this book—and the result is a model that can be used in practice.

An editorial board gave us assistance as well as advice. Face-to-face and through e-mail, we had many discussions on the relationship between architecture in real life and in DYA. For this, we owe thanks to Harold ten Böhmer (Ohra), Jan Machiel Dalebout (DaimlerChrysler Services), Frans van Dijk (Zilveren Kruis), Stella van Dijk (Wehkamp), Frank Howldar (RVS Verzekeringen), Rob Jansen (Interpolis), Ad van Kelle (MCB International), Marten Kramer (AMEV Nederland), Ron Linssen (ABN AMRO Lease Holding), John Mulders (Belastingdienst Automatiseringscentrum), Walter Smit (SNS Reaal Verzekeringen), Johan Snijder (Buma/Stemra/Cedar), Kees Tuijnman (SNS Reaal Verzekeringen), Bert de Wals (Postbank), and Leo Wiegel (PCM). We are pleased to note that a number of the above-mentioned organizations have actually introduced DYA in their everyday practices.

In addition to this editorial board, we also benefited from the advice, mainly in the conceptual field, of the Committee of Recommendation. The committee included Jan Hoogervorst (KLM), Vincent Rikkerink (Fortis Bank), Theo Thiadens (University of Twente), and Han Wagter (Kappa Holding). We are very grateful for their inspiration.

It goes without saying that we also received a great deal of help and support from within our own organization. Many of our colleagues read draft versions of this book and gave us their comments. Our contacts in the Sogeti Nederland B.V. management team were Nijs Blokland, Maarten Galesloot, and Jeroen Versteeg. They have always given us their help and support. We want to thank all our colleagues for their contributions. Without you, we would never have achieved this!

We are very pleased to have our book translated into English, enabling us to reach an even larger audience. We want to thank our colleagues of Sogeti, Jeroen Versteeg, and Klaas Brongers, for making this translation possible and Sabine Bolkenstijn and Allan Reid for assisting us in preparing this translation.

We wish you, the reader, much pleasure when you read this book and apply DYA in practice. Naturally, we are very interested in your experiences with architecture and DYA in particular. Please submit any reactions and experiences by e-mail to *dya@sogeti.nl*.

We are convinced that you too can improve your business using IT. This book can help you do just that!

> Roel Wagter
> Martin van den Berg
> Joost Luijpers
> Marlies van Steenbergen

INTRODUCTION

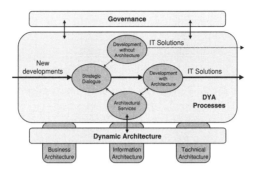

Information technology—IT—plays an ever-growing role in our daily lives and for many organizations IT is critical in reaching their business objectives. Effective and efficient use of IT is therefore paramount and any organization that makes incorrect or expensive use of IT will experience negative effects immediately. Optimum use of IT within an organization does not, however, happen spontaneously: Choices need to be made and there are agreements to be reached. Architecture is an important tool in making the right decisions and reaching the necessary agreements. It provides an overview of the alternatives and adds a high degree of consistency to the agreements made.

Designing enterprise architecture on paper does not bring an organization any closer to more efficient and effective use of IT, nor does it help the organization achieve its business objectives any faster. The enterprise architecture needs to become an integral part of—and be supported by—the organization as a whole. An architect should continually ask him- or herself: When should I design which part of the architecture, with whom should I consult in doing this, and what will happen with the results?

TARGET AUDIENCE

This book presents an approach to enterprise architecture that enables organizations to achieve their business objectives not only faster, but also with a higher degree of proficiency. Key elements in this approach are multidisciplinary teams, purposeful architectural design, and room for deliberate noncompliance to the standard architecture. These elements are brought together in a model called *Dynamic Architecture* (DYA).

3

The DYA model is built around three distinct processes that provide an organization with the full benefits of using architecture:

- *Strategic Dialogue*, in which the company's business objectives are determined and, after due consideration, are further defined as project proposals.
- *Development with Architecture*, in which the IT solutions are implemented.
- *Architectural Services*, which supports the other two processes with principles, guidelines, and models.

To ensure that these processes are implemented correctly and continue to function successfully, a certain amount of management is necessary. This facet of the architectural process is also dealt with by the DYA model. The underlying basis for our model is Dynamic Architecture, which has been specifically devised with the speed of change in mind.

The objective of the DYA model and of this book is to provide you with concrete methods for implementing and professionalizing the architectural processes within your own organization. The ultimate goal is to enable the enterprise architecture to make a major contribution to achieving the business objectives of your organization. It is for the person who asks himself: "How can I raise the level of architectural awareness and architectural integration in my organization to such an extent that IT will be used to better effect?"

The DYA model is an answer to a practical need and is based on many years of practical experience in designing and developing enterprise architectures. During this time, it became increasingly clear that the bottleneck in successful deployment of IT is not that we do not know how to develop effective enterprise architecture, but that the architecture itself is not sufficiently integrated into and supported by the organization. This is the reason why we discuss neither a specific form of enterprise architecture nor the necessary steps to achieve any specific type of architecture in this book. We believe that a method for developing enterprise architecture is no longer the greatest obstacle.

Indeed, we refer you to some of these methods, including James Martin's Information Strategy Planning, the META Group's Enterprise Architecture Strategies Process, and Integrated Architecture Framework of Capgemini.[1] What we want to demonstrate is that these methods can be used to better effect and with more success by securely anchoring the entire architectural development process within an organization. By embedding one of them or a similar method into the DYA model, you can effectively prevent the products of your architectural process from turning into a "paper tiger."

THE STRUCTURE OF THIS BOOK

How to raise the level of architectural awareness and integration is presented in nine chapters:

- *Chapter 1* discusses the role of IT in the present time and the consequences of this role. We show that there is an increasing demand on IT departments to produce more agility and coherence in respect of IT solutions.

- *Chapter 2* shows that standard IT responses to a request for more agility and coherence just provide the answer to one side of the question: either agility (with new development methods and standard software) or coherence (architecture).

- *Chapter 3* illustrates that the concept of dynamic architecture fulfills the need to increase both agility and coherence while ensuring that they stay in balance. It also provides a sketch of the characteristics of dynamic architecture.

- *Chapter 4* deals with the components of the DYA model and the principles that led to its construction. This chapter gives the reader a first impression of the model.

- *Chapter 5* provides an in-depth description of the model's first process, the Strategic Dialogue. During the Strategic Dialogue, an organization determines the company's business objectives, checks their feasibility in a business case and, after due consideration, further defines them as project proposals.

- *Chapter 6* discusses the model's second main process, Architectural Services. Architectural Services provides the necessary architectures "just enough, just in time."

- *Chapter 7* highlights the model's third process, Development with Architecture. In this process, IT solutions are designed, built, and implemented. Normally, these developments are carried out within the Architectural Framework, but under exceptional circumstances, there is room for deliberate non-compliance to the standard architecture.

- *Chapter 8* examines the management aspects of architecture.

- *Chapter 9* concludes with a recapitulation of the main points made in previous chapters.

To illustrate both the model and the different effects that result from choosing either to employ or not to employ architecture, we introduce a fictitious company called TeleBel in Chapter 5. TeleBel is a telecommunications company that provides telecommunication services to the general public. TeleBel does not own a telephone network, but buys the required services from other telecom operators. One of the current projects being developed for TeleBel is WWW-TeleBel. The object of WWW-TeleBel is to provide TeleBel customers on the Internet with information about their use of the traditional TeleBel telephone service. In Chapters 5 through 8, you will find descriptions of the situation at TeleBel and, in particular, the progress of the WWW-TeleBel project.

During our presentation and subsequent discussion of the DYA processes, we will also introduce techniques and tools to effectively support these processes. These techniques and tools will be introduced in a separate section in which we use the situation at TeleBel to illustrate the application of the technique or tool in question. A number of tools will be explained in greater detail in a concrete example that takes the form of an "Intermezzo" at the end of the chapter in which the tool is introduced. These intermezzos are independent of the rest of the chapter and merely illustrate the various elements of the tool being explained. We chose to keep these examples relatively simple and understandable rather than strive for completeness.

Note

1. For Martin's Information Strategy Planning, see J.L Simons and G.M.A. Verheijen, *Informatiestrategie als Managementopgave: Planning, Ontwikkeling en Beheer van Informatieverzorging op Basis van Information Engineering* [Information Strategy as Management Task: Planning, Development and Control of Information Provision Based on Information Engineering] (Deventer, Netherlands: Stenfert Kroese/ Kluwer Bedrijfswetenschappen, 1991). For the Enterprise Architecture Strategies Process, see META Group, "EAS Process Model: Evolution 2000" (META Group, April 2000); and B. Tuft, "Enterprise Architecture: Laying the e-Foundation for 21st-Century Business" (paper presented at Congress META Group, March 27–29, 2000, Munich). For the Integrated Architecture Framework of CAP Gemini Ernst & Young, see J. Dietz , P. Mallens, H. Goedvolk, and D. Rijsenbrij, "A Conceptual Framework for the Continuous Alignment of Business and ICT" (Technische Universiteit Delft and Cap Gemini, December 1999); and V. Van Swede, "Information Architecture: Relevance and Use as a Business-IT Alignment Tool" (Cap Gemini Institute, 1999).

CHAPTER 1

Agility and Coherence: A Conflict of Interests?

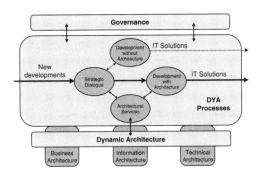

POTENTIAL OF INFORMATION TECHNOLOGY

The importance of information technology (IT) has continually increased throughout the last decades. At the present level almost everyone makes use of IT daily, whether they realize it or not. In the pioneering days of IT, it was mainly used to ease the burden of repetitive administrative tasks. Today, IT creates new tasks and services and allows completely new business models to be designed. The most obvious examples are current developments concerning the Internet and e-business.

IT has great potential for influencing markets. It bridges time and distance in a completely new way, and opens markets that were previously unattainable because they were geographically too remote. Until recently, a small town would have no more than three banks competing with each other for the business of the town's residents. Today, we have a situation in which literally thousands of national and international banks compete with each other for customers in that same small town. Financial institutions, such as banks, no longer have to maintain a physical presence to be able to do business. Financial transactions, such as buying and selling shares, are being executed electronically and the customer can monitor the progress of such transactions on his or her personal Internet page. In 2000, more than half of all stock orders placed by individuals in the United States were initiated via the Internet.

In addition, IT has a great potential for expanding cooperation between individual units within an organization. E-mail has become the standard mode of communication and working from home has become a topical issue because of the progress that IT has made in remote communications. At the same time, we see that organizations are beginning to join forces in several new ways. A number of organizations are actively engaged in setting up electronic marketplaces for commerce between companies (B2B, i.e., business-to-business commerce). An example is the Covisint initiative by Ford, General Motors, DaimlerChrysler, Renault, and Nissan.

IT also creates the possibility of shaping products and services to the exact requirements of the consumer. A number of car manufacturers are so far advanced with their information systems that they can provide interim progress reports to customers on the production and delivery scheme of their new cars. The customer has the opportunity to use an e-mail form on a webpage to change the color and the accessories of the car while it is being manufactured. A customer, therefore, can get fully involved (online and interactively) in the internal processes of the manufacturer.

The examples above illustrate the potential of IT. Our challenge is to realize this potential: through effective and efficient use of IT.

USING IT: A PROBLEM IN THE MAKING?

In everyday practice, effective and efficient use of IT is more of a challenge than one would expect. Many companies and organizations have difficulty in achieving effective and efficient use of their IT systems. We, the authors, are regularly confronted with this difficulty in our everyday dealings with companies and organizations.

An example is the debacle which took place around Christmas 1999 in the United States, when many Americans did their Christmas shopping via the Internet. Ordering presents using a website and a browser proved to be less of a challenge than most people expected, but unfortunately delivering the presents was a completely different story. Most of the Internet stores failed to deliver on time, the websites for ordering were perfect, whereas the logistic process for delivery was unable to cope.

There are more examples of the difficulties that companies have in using IT efficiently and effectively. Recently, customers of a telecommunications company received a reminder that they should pay their telephone bills promptly or face being cut off. To say the least, this was a strange state of affairs. The customers always paid their bill automatically using a "Direct Debit" facility. To be on the safe side, several customers undoubtedly paid the reminder. Several days later, it became apparent that the automatic debit payments had not been processed on time and, therefore, the next process in the chain of events automatically began to produce reminders. Consequently, a malfunction in the billing system wrongly accused a great number of customers of being overdue with their payments. The company had a lot of explaining to do!

Roger Moore's Bank Account Made Public

Zurich–Due to an error at a Swiss bank, Internet users were able to view the account information of the actor Roger Moore, the singer Udo Jurgens, and thousands of other celebrity customers. In addition to bank account numbers and financial transactions, the private addresses of these wealthy customers were also viewable on the Internet.

According to a spokesman of Credit Suisse, the sensitive information was accidentally placed on the pages of their Internet bank facility Direct Net. The information remained there a week for the world to see.

Source: *Eindhovens Dagblad* (daily newspaper), November 10, 2000.

These are the visible effects of the problems that afflict many organizations and with which they have been struggling for some time. People in such organizations often ask themselves the same questions:

- How can I link up my applications so that the right information is available at the correct time and place?
- How can I shorten the time needed to produce new functionality so that the time-to-market for new products and services is correspondingly reduced?

- How can I lower my maintenance and support costs?

- How can I manage and organize my IT services so that I can outsource parts of it?

- How can I bring my project portfolio under control so that the relationships and dependencies between various IT initiatives are clarified and I can deploy my budget for IT to a better purpose?

Remarkably enough, we already know the answers to all these questions. We know how to link applications—for example, by using middleware. The quest for flexibility and reduction of development time is being answered by the component paradigm that shows great promise for further development. Maintenance and support costs can be reduced by a drastic reduction in the number of hardware platforms and development environments within an organization.

So why do we not use our hard-earned knowledge and solve all these problems?

AGILITY AND COHERENCE

We certainly have sufficient answers to the problems mentioned above but, unfortunately, we do not always put them into practice. This is mainly because we are not given enough time to do so. There always seems to be another urgent problem that needs an ad hoc solution, frustrating all our well thought plans and improvements.

Questions about sharing information, managing the number of development environments, and linking applications are all questions about *coherence*. Coherence is necessary to ensure the correct interaction of the various business processes and to allow the organization to present itself as a uniform entity. To obtain coherence, we need to consider the functioning of the organization as a whole, including its information systems. This means investigation, reaching consensus and planning. Such activities take time.

At the same time, the market demands *agility*. Products become obsolete at an alarming rate—for example, we can barely keep up with the pace at which new types of cell phones are being introduced. Also, customers expect an answer to their e-mail messages within 24 hours and expect products to be delivered within a day of ordering.

One of the main reasons for this is that the traditional barriers to entering a certain marketplace, such as time and distance, are constantly being eroded. As a result, competition increases. In addition, at a growing rate, the competitive edge is being provided by information and information systems. These can be copied easily. In a relatively short time, a competitive edge gained in this way can be effectively combated. This means that the advantage is short-lived and companies must seek new advantages more rapidly. In short, business keeps unfolding at an ever increasing pace, thanks to the new opportunities offered by IT and, as a result, the IT organization has to work even faster to keep up with the business.

In the 1970s and 1980s, business processes were redesigned on average once every seven years. This rate of change was easy for the IT department to follow. The time needed to alter the information systems that supported new or changed business processes stayed within acceptable limits. In the 1990s, the rate of change began to increase and information systems began to lag behind. In 2000, a manager succinctly remarked: "We can completely redesign our business processes every three months and subsequently our IT department needs a year to catch up with the supporting information systems."

What we encounter repeatedly in this kind of situation are the contradictory demands of agility and coherence. If we want to accomplish something quickly, we apparently have too little time to achieve consensus with others on what we would like to do or to make detailed plans about what we want to do. However, if someone considers aspects other than his or her immediate interests, he or she may decide not to follow the most direct route in achieving his goal, thus using more time than is strictly necessary. This tension between agility and coherence is perhaps best illustrated by examining the opinions of the traditional supporters of coherence and those of agility with regard to each other. In an insurance company, the architects, who are primarily engaged in ensuring that coherence has the highest priority, are regarded as "professional decelerators" by the development teams. The architects, in their turn, never fail to remark on the latest "quick and dirty" solution provided by the developers. These opposing views are reflected in Exhibit 1.1, which illustrates that the process of achieving business objectives by developing IT solutions is influenced by the two demands of agility and coherence.

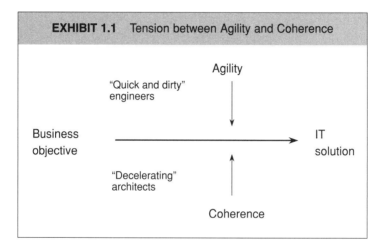

EXHIBIT 1.1   Tension between Agility and Coherence

INCREASING TENSION

The tension between agility and coherence is becoming greater. We have observed that IT has permeated to the very roots of organizations and is becoming increasingly important for them as a whole. Where previously IT was only one of the many tools used to achieve business objectives, it has become crucial to many organizations. During the last 10 years, IT has made a major contribution to the progressive integration of the supply chain (e.g., organizations, their suppliers, and their customers). This is illustrated in Exhibit 1.2.

In the past, the relationship between businesses, suppliers, and customers was clearly demarcated. Within a company, employees, processes, and information systems were integrated to a certain

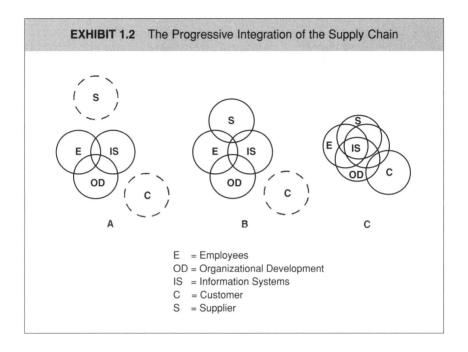

EXHIBIT 1.2 The Progressive Integration of the Supply Chain

E = Employees
OD = Organizational Development
IS = Information Systems
C = Customer
S = Supplier

extent. However, the customers and suppliers played no active part in the company's business processes.

Several years ago, the relationship evolved into that shown in Exhibit 1.2(B). Suppliers were no longer behaving as separate entities; and they made a clear move toward becoming a more or less integral part of a company's internal supply chain. This progress toward more integration was initiated by the arrival of *electronic data interchange* (EDI) several years beforehand. The supply chain that resulted from this integration between supplier and business led to more efficient business processes for both companies. For example, immediately after a six-pack of beer is paid for at the supermarket, the automatic stock control system of the supermarket places an order at the brewery for another six-pack. Stocks at the supermarket are kept to a minimum, and the brewery's processes are geared to produce the optimum amount of beer. The Internet has encouraged an even greater use of this trend for supplier integration.

At the same time, customers are moving closer to businesses. Telebanking and customers monitoring the manufacture of their new cars are good examples of customer integration. These trends will continue to evolve and the three parties will merge even further, resulting in an integrated relationship, as illustrated in Exhibit 1.2(C). Supplier, customer, and business form a close network within which both the supplier and the customer have a direct influence on the business processes of the company. This far-reaching supply chain integration is made possible by IT.

If we consider such developments further, we can conclude that IT is no longer just supportive to the business, but that it has become an integral part of the business itself, and has, as a result, a direct influence on the financial success of an enterprise. The influence of IT does not stop here. IT today enables completely new business models to be devised and implemented. The online auctioning and group buying models are examples of business models that have been created on the basis of modern IT techniques.[1]

An online auction house such as eBay creates a virtual meeting place for supply and demand and enables a bargaining process in cyberspace so that potential buyers can bid against each other to buy any of the offered items. This business model is only made possible by virtue of the Internet. The Internet removes the traditional geographical barriers, enabling many more people to take part in the auction. The essence of the group-buying model is the accumulation of the demand for a certain product. *Group buyers* try to bring together as many potential individual buyers for a certain product as possible and combine their orders to negotiate a volume discount from the sellers. Bringing potential buyers together is made possible by using the Internet—without it, the group-buying model could not have been realized.

In addition to these new forms of enterprise, we increasingly see well-established organizations using IT to offer new services and to open new markets. IT has gained strategic importance for the enterprise. Previously, IT strategy was defined as a direct result of business strategy. Today, business strategy and IT strategy have so many common interests and objectives that they frequently overlap and should be developed simultaneously, as illustrated in Exhibit 1.3.

The possibilities created by IT are increasingly responsible for the direction chosen in determining a business strategy. E-business is currently the best example of how IT can determine the business strategy of an enterprise. Almost all enterprises are or will be involved in doing business on the "information superhighway," either directly, because they have taken the plunge and are developing their own plans for e-business, or indirectly, because their traditional marketplace is being gradually eroded and replaced by an electronic version.

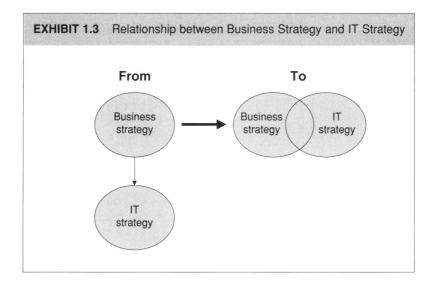

EXHIBIT 1.3 Relationship between Business Strategy and IT Strategy

What is becoming increasingly evident, especially in respect to e-business, are the heavier demands on both agility and coherence due to increased transparency of the market. Customers can now easily compare which supplier offers the best deal. Internet sites can be found where the prices, terms, and conditions of the various suppliers of almost any kind of product can be conveniently compared, enabling consumers to select the supplier that best suits their needs. Insurance policies, books, CDs, vacation packages, and many other products can be compared in this way using the Internet.

The pace of change in the marketplace has increased rapidly and the effects of these changes are becoming more widespread. The moment that an enterprise brings a new product into the market, it is immediately visible to a potential customer and he or she can immediately react to this new product. In order not to lose customers, the competition will also have to act swiftly. This leads to a rapidly evolving and increasingly aggressive market, in which customers are supported in their decision making by completely new tools such as search engines and intelligent agents.

The increased transparency of the market also results in increased demands on coherence. The ease with which consumers can compare products and services means that a company should only offer those in which it excels. A product that is too expensive or a service which only offers half a solution is a waste of effort. The company must ensure that it can keep the promises it makes to its customers. One single wrong step and the customer is gone! He or she can easily find alternatives. This requires that the internal business processes are properly attuned to each other and that there is a clear understanding of mutual expectations within the organization. In addition to the increase in competitiveness, we see that organizations are once again concentrating on their core business and that less profitable activities are being contracted out to partners. This results in network organizations that are in fact an extension of the development illustrated in Exhibit 1.2, adding the *P* for partner. Together with partners, an organization will continually search for ways to increase the value-for-money of its products and services. The most distinctive characteristics of a network organization are (1) continually changing internal and external affiliations and (2) shifting organizational boundaries because of flexible in- and outsourcing in reaction to the opportunities that arise. IT is no longer purely an internal affair. To a great extent, IT determines the effectiveness of collaborating within a partnership ("from IT to exT").

In all this, we recognize an increasing importance of IT and a corresponding increase in the tension between agility and coherence. Both are essential conditions for an efficient and effective IT use, but both conditions must be held in balance.

If the balance is tipped in favor of agility, costs will rise astronomically; partners will no longer be aware of what the others are doing; key information will no longer be available; the customer in search of information will be "sent from pillar to post"; and it will be increasingly difficult to introduce good products and services into the market.

If the balance is tipped in favor of coherence, the organization runs the risk of creating the best products and services on the market, but making them available for sale far too late. The customer either no longer needs the product or has already chosen from one of the competitors.

THE CHALLENGE

The challenge facing the modern organization is finding the correct balance between coherence and agility. The object of this book is to help organizations solve this puzzle and find that balance. Later in the book, we examine the answers that have already been found for the increasing demands for both agility and coherence. Because these answers focus on only one side of the scale (either agility or coherence), there is no answer yet for how to achieve a continuing balance between the two forces. Therefore, the lion's share of this publication will be dedicated to providing an answer to this urgent question. As a first step, the idea of Dynamic Architecture must be introduced and developed into a practical model. This model, by keeping agility and coherence in balance, helps utilize IT to such an extent that its full potential in helping to achieve business objectives will be realized.

Note

1. C. Holland, H. Bouwman, and M. Smidts, "Back to the Bottom Line: Onderzoek naar succesvolle e-businessmodellen" [Back to the Bottom Line: Investigation of Successful E-Business Models] (ECP.NL, 2001).

CHAPTER 2

Agility and Coherence Considered Separately

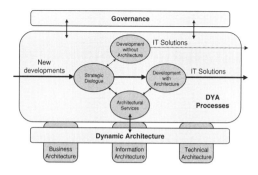

DIFFERENT ANSWERS TO DIFFERENT QUESTIONS

Chapter 1 established that there is an ever-increasing emphasis on the necessity for agility and coherence in the development of an IT solution. The IT world has created several responses to this necessity. These responses are aimed at accelerating the IT development process or at improving the coordination between individual IT developments. Acceleration of the development process is being sought in employing new development methods or in implementing standard packages, while improving coordination between developments is being sought in development under architectural guidance.

INCREASING AGILITY:
NEW DEVELOPMENT METHODS

To increase the speed at which applications are constructed, several new IT development methods have been created such as DSDM (Dynamic Systems Development Method) and XP (eXtreme Programming). These new methods set aside the many and often complex principles used by the more traditional approach and replace them with fewer and less-complicated principles.

An important aspect of DSDM is the time-box principle. *Time-boxing* is based on the precept that a definite and unchangeable deadline is set for a project and within this deadline a certain goal must be achieved. Irrespective of what happens during the course of the project, the deadline remains unchanged. If the deadline is endangered in any way, it will not be postponed, but certain aspects of the functionality will be sacrificed instead. This is based on the assumption that a usable and significant part of the system (around 80%) can be constructed in 20% of the time needed to build the complete system. An essential part of time-boxing is a constant evaluation of the priority of each functional requirement. To ensure that, at the least, a usable system will be produced, delivery of a minimum set of requirements is guaranteed. The remaining requirements are, in theory, exchangeable for time and money.

XP also makes use of time-boxing by defining a number of iterations. In a "planning game" between development staff, management, and end users, a decision is taken as to which parts of the application should be realized and in which iteration.

Both DSDM and XP take into account that user requirements may change during the development process. This is supported by "just-in-time" planning and by ensuring that parts of the system are not created before they are needed: Detailed plans are drawn up when necessary and not beforehand, and functionality is only built at the precise moment that it is necessary for the progress of the project. In this way, these methods ensure that, within the limits of time and money, a system will be delivered that complies with the current requirements of the users.

DSDM and XP are just two examples of new development methods that focus on increasing the speed of the development process. Other methods exist with this focus and, without a doubt, more will follow. In general, these new methods show a great deal of promise, and it appears that they can produce a usable result in less time than more traditional development methods. They form an adequate line of action in the quest for more agility.

Such new development methods are aimed at quickly producing IT solutions, targeted at a specific business goal. They do not concern themselves with the question as to how the solution will relate to and cope with other events within the organization. They do not give any guarantee in respect of coherence.

In addition to the use of new development methods, organizations are trying to introduce more agility in the development process by implementing standard software solutions. The rationale underlying this course of action is that standard software is an "off-the-shelf" solution and, therefore, needs no further development. This should lead to quicker implementation. There is, however, a certain nuance needed depending on the type of package being implemented:

- *Software packages in the form of a programmable framework.* In general, these packages offer a solution for a specific "niche" market and can be easily tailored to meet user needs (e.g., Broadvision and Silverstream). They offer a framework for constructing Web-based applications and provide all the necessary code and facilities for handling Web-based dialogues with end users. These packages effectively reduce the necessary development time because part of the required functionality is already provided by the package itself. Largely because these packages support a restricted part of the business process, they can be quickly adapted to the needs of the business and implemented without a great deal of effort.

- *Companywide or so-called Enterprise Resource Planning (ERP) solutions.* ERP packages are rich in functionality. For example, ERP implementations such as SAP, Oracle, PeopleSoft, and Baan can support most of the business processes of a company whose emphasis is on the production of goods. Practically speaking, however, implementing such a package should not be taken lightly. Implementing an ERP solution often takes just as long as or even longer than implementing a tailor-made solution.

Standard software solutions in themselves do not offer a guarantee of coherence. Just like the tailor-made solution, packages must be integrated into the organization's existing set of information systems (even ERP solutions do not cover all of a company's information needs). In practice, this often proves to be a complex issue and frequently forms the bottleneck in an implementation trajectory.

INCREASING COHERENCE: ARCHITECTURAL AWARENESS

Many organizations attempt to achieve enhanced coherence in their IT developments by improving the architectural awareness of the organization. *Architecture*, in this context, is the consistent set of rules and models that guide the design and implementation of processes, organizational structures, information flows, and the technical infrastructure within an organization. Architecture can be considered as a set of agreements that ensure that individual developments interface correctly with each other and with overall company interests. Indeed, by clearly outlining the scope of a development project, its responsibilities, and its domain, the freedom as well as the restrictions of the individual project team are established. Products delivered by a project team that is compliant with the architecture will always fit within the greater context of business needs.

Improving architectural awareness is clearly an answer to the increased necessity for greater coherence in IT developments within an organization. In practice, however, complying with architecture is not an easy matter. We mentioned earlier that architects are perceived as a restraining influence, and this bears witness to the difficulties that architects face. All too often, an architect's efforts result in piles of paper that are of no practical use to a project team and, instead of being used, immediately disappear in some drawer. Being compliant with the architecture is seen by most project participants as restrictive: The project team is constrained in its freedom of choice and receives nothing in return. Business owners and managers also perceive architects as meddlesome: No sooner have they developed a brilliant idea for a new business opportunity, than one of the architects tells them their idea is impossible to achieve within the architecture.

Even those who see the direct benefits of using architecture are confronted with the fact that compliance with architecture costs a great deal of valuable time, and, therefore, they often decide that, just this once, architecture will be set aside. Their excuse is that the market demands an immediate response and there is insufficient time to wait for architecture.

> The development department has hired an expert to design a planning system. Having delivered a detailed design for the system, the expert offers to program the system as well. Taking the scarcity of IT experts into consideration, the department makes grateful use of this offer. Using the expert, the project can progress as planned. However, the expert can only work in a development environment that is not part of the company's IT platform policy. In spite of this, the department decides to go ahead, and the desire to continue to make progress prevails once again.

In brief, compliance with architecture is recognized as an answer to the necessity for coherence; but, at the same time, it is seen as a hindrance in the IT development process.

This is a bitter pill to swallow because architecture not only offers an answer to the need for coherence, but it is also essential in achieving agility. If, for example, an organization agrees that data should only be registered once and that functionality should be uniquely assigned among the various information systems, then changes in the informational needs of the company can be realized much more quickly—that is, changes only need to be made in one system instead of many.

> A company decided to carry out an internal survey to determine the reasons behind the maintenance needed to upgrade their information systems. The survey surprisingly revealed the result that most of this effort was caused by changes in other, interfacing, systems.

The promise of architecture is, therefore, great. Nevertheless, why does architectural guidance prove to be so difficult to put into practice? The main reason for this is in the origins of IT architecture. The practice of designing architecture began at the same time as the appearance of traditional information planning. Traditional information planning commenced when the world could be described as less dynamic than in the present. Both the market and the internal business processes changed less frequently, and IT had a far less important role in the business than is customary today.

The goal of traditional information planning was to create an information plan that outlined how in future information was to be supplied and, moreover, the steps required to create this future information situation. Both IT and the business assumed and accepted that carrying out the information plan would take three to five years. Presently, an organization's planning horizon is much shorter and does not allow the luxury of so much time for carrying out an extensive plan. The linear, project-driven approach is no longer acceptable because, as soon as the plans are finished, they are obsolete. Trying to predict the needs of a company for the next three years has become practically impossible.

In the traditional approach to information planning, IT was considered to be of secondary importance to the company's strategy. First, the company's overall strategy was decided at the highest business level, and, subsequently, the IT department filled in the IT strategy based on the overall strategy. Architecture, in such a context, is purely an internal affair for the IT department, and the business neither feels nor wants any part of the responsibility for determining the IT strategy. In the era in which we now live, and in which IT has become of strategic importance in conducting business, such an attitude is no longer viable. To adequately react to each and every opportunity in the marketplace, business and IT strategy must be considered as a single entity, and the responsibility for determining these strategies must be carried by both business and IT.

In the planned approach, which typifies traditional information planning, a comprehensive architecture for the entire organization had to be designed and approved before any one part of the architecture could be realized. This almost always resulted in the aforementioned mountains of unread paper. The autonomous project team had designed the architecture with little or no input from the user organization and the end product, the architecture, was isolated from the everyday questions and challenges facing the organization.

Finally, existing methods for information planning are built around the assumption that, once the architecture has been designed, all problems have been addressed and that nothing stands in the way of realization. The emphasis of the architecture project lies in delivering the goods, in this case the architecture. Rarely is any consideration given to the thought that the method used for developing the architecture should be embedded into the business change process of the organization. Short-term solutions to problems that appear suddenly often require exceptional measures, and these measures, just as often, do not fit into the prescribed architecture. This fact of life is often ignored by the architecture project team. This means the architecture is not seen as an integral part of the dynamics of the organization and is ignored at every opportunity.

There is a discrepancy between the precepts that led to the introduction of architectural awareness and the demands of the present time. This is illustrated in Exhibit 2.1. The increased dynamics

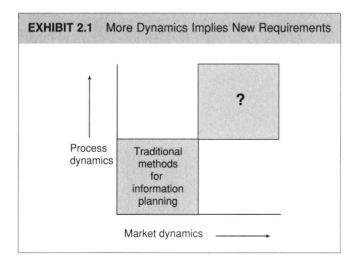

EXHIBIT 2.1   More Dynamics Implies New Requirements

Process dynamics

Traditional methods for information planning

?

Market dynamics

of the market and business processes demand a new approach to architecture.

ONE ANSWER TO BOTH QUESTIONS: DYNAMIC ARCHITECTURE

The answer to the desire for more agility is being sought in new development methods—and the answer to the need for more coherence is being sought in architectural awareness. However, new development methods, which provide an increase in agility, do not bring any guarantee of coherence, and architectural awareness, which should provide for coherence, is perceived as being a hindrance to progress and, moreover, proves difficult to implement.

What is missing is a solution that combines both aspects, and the answer is to be found in a combination of both a new development method *and* architecture. This, in turn, demands a new approach to architecture. Working under architectural guidance must no longer be seen as synonymous with wasting time. Rather, it should become synonymous with *gaining* time. In the next chapters, a new approach to architecture, Dynamic Architecture, is presented that is explicitly aimed at achieving business goals quickly in a constantly changing environment. The principle behind Dynamic Architecture is not another explanation of how to design architecture—there are enough professional architects today who know how to do that. Dynamic Architecture is about the positioning and embedding of architecture at the right level within an organization. That is, which architecture is to be designed at what moment and for what purpose, who is involved in the design process, and who is going to use the architecture and to what end.

The questions posed are:

- How can we bridge the gap between strategy and realization?
- How can we create agility without returning to ad hoc work and chaos?

- How can we ensure that all IT developments contribute to achieving the business goals?

We look for the answers to these questions in a combination of joint strategy-forming by business and IT, a purposeful approach to architecture and recognizing three different development strategies. But first, we need to examine the notion of dynamic architecture closely in the next chapter.

CHAPTER 3

Dynamic Architecture

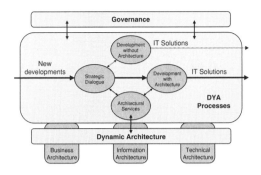

WANTED: AGILE ARCHITECTURE

Architecture has proven to be an indispensable asset for an organization in reaching its business objectives. Without employing architecture, only the smallest of organizations are exempt from the unmanageable tangle of IT development environments, hardware platforms, software applications, and projects. As a further consequence, the lack of architecture allows the cost of IT development and maintenance to rise. In this scenario, the organization becomes insufficiently equipped to react to market developments and incapable of quickly taking action in the pursuit of its objectives.

Architecture has an essential role in creating the ability to react and providing an organization with the capacity to respond to changes in the market, even in situations when such changes cannot be predicted. In doing so, however, architecture itself must undergo a number of changes. What we need is an *agile* architecture, an architecture that has been specifically designed to facilitate the speed of change. This chapter will explain what this entails.

ARCHITECTURE: A MULTIFACETED CONCEPT

Architecture is a concept with many facets and can almost be all things to all people. Our interpretation, perception, and understanding of architecture will not necessarily be the same as that of our colleagues. A unique, unilaterally accepted definition of architecture has not yet been established. This need not be a problem, as long as we are aware of the differences in interpretation and make them explicit in our communication.

Where do these differences in interpretation arise? When we discuss architecture, there are three aspects that must be clarified beforehand—otherwise, confusion and misunderstanding can result:

1. Chronology
2. Context or subject matter
3. Level of abstraction

There is a chronological aspect to architecture. We have encountered the following (chronological) definitions of architecture:

- A description of the current situation
- A blueprint for a desired future situation
- A set of guidelines for carrying out changes

The Gartner Group makes this even more explicit (in terms of time) by identifying the above definitions as three forms of architecture: the *today* architecture, the *tomorrow* architecture, and the *next-minute* architecture. These three forms are represented in Exhibit 3.1.

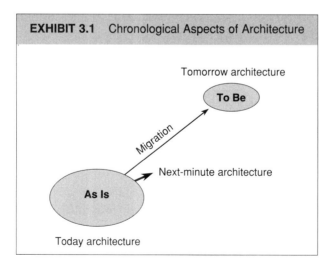

EXHIBIT 3.1   Chronological Aspects of Architecture

It is easy to imagine that a great deal of confusion can arise when the type of architecture is not made explicit in a specific situation.

The aspect of context, or subject matter, also needs to be explained. Architecture, as a concept, can be applied to different contexts or subject matter. Architecture can be developed for products and services, processes, organizational structures, information, applications, middleware, platforms, and networks. This creates product-and-services architecture, process architecture, organizational architecture, information architecture, and so on.

The various architectural domains are often grouped together to form three main types of architecture:

1. Business architecture

2. Information architecture

3. Technical architecture

Business architecture sketches the contours for the way in which an organization can be structured to effectively pursue its business objectives. Business architecture consists of three domains: (1) the products and services offered; (2) the processes responsible for producing these products and services; and (3) the organizational structure required to carry out these processes.

Information architecture sketches the design contours for the provision of information within an organization. It consists of two domains: (1) the data that is important for the correct functioning of the organization; and (2) the applications that ensure that this information is correctly distributed within the organization.

Technical architecture sketches the contours of the technical infrastructure necessary to support the organization. It consists of three domains: (1) the hardware platforms; (2) the network components; and (3) the software required for information sharing between applications (also known as *middleware*).

Exhibit 3.2 illustrates the constituent parts—that is, the architectural domains—of the three types of architecture.

EXHIBIT 3.2 Architectural Types and Domains

Business architecture	Information architecture	Technical architecture
• Product/service architecture • Process architecture • Organization architecture	• Data architecture • Application architecture	• Middleware architecture • Platform architecture • Network architecture

---

Finally, different levels of abstraction can be distinguished when talking about architecture. An organization can issue the following statement: "Our customers have one single point of contact for all questions." This visionary statement (i.e., general principle) provides direction for a variety of organizational decisions and can be justifiably called an architectural decision. It also leads to several more concrete policy guidelines such as "customer information must be stored centrally" and "call center employees are trained both broadly and in-depth." These statements (i.e., rules and guidelines) are also part of the architecture, but at a different level. The rules and guidelines can be detailed further in models, creating, for example, a data model for customer information and a profile sketch for call center employees. Such models also form part of the architecture at yet another level. Exhibit 3.3 illustrates the various levels.

Clearly, in everyday practice, the concept of architecture manifests itself in several guises. Despite all these different appearances, the prime concept remains the same: Choices have to be made; agree-

---

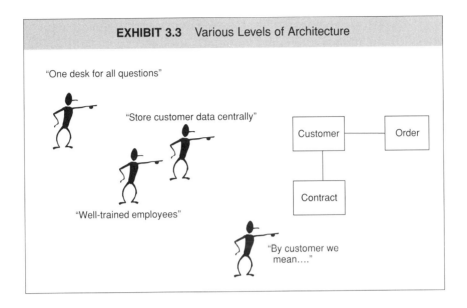

EXHIBIT 3.3 Various Levels of Architecture

"One desk for all questions"

"Store customer data centrally"

"Well-trained employees"

"By customer we mean...."

Customer — Order

Contract

ments have to be reached; policy has to be decided; and the end result should be the attainment of business objectives.

In all further references to architecture in this book, the following is meant by the term *architecture*:

> The consistent set of rules and models that guide the design and implementation of processes, organizational structures, information flows, and the technical infrastructure within an organization.[1]

From this definition it should be clear that a great deal of emphasis is placed on "Next-Minute Architecture"—that is, architecture as a tool to give direction to design and implementation. From this point of view, architecture can be seen as a management tool that gives direction to the change processes within an organization. To this end, architecture consists of principles, norms, guidelines, standards, and models. By using this definition, architecture can cover an entire perspective, from business architecture to technical architecture, and several levels within architecture can be distinguished, from general to specific principles and detailed models.

In providing such a broad definition of architecture, we by no means imply that the implementation of architecture within an organization should be as widespread as possible. On the contrary, a minimalist approach in designing architecture is advocated: Do not develop more architecture than your organization needs.

DYNAMIC ARCHITECTURE: ARCHITECTURE AIMED AT AGILITY

From the previous sections, it is easy to imagine that architecture, considered from an agility perspective, can easily get a bad image. Architects can be totally occupied with filling in the numerous details of an architecture and lose sight of the prime purpose of architecture: Helping the business to achieve its objectives. After months of incubation, that "paper tiger," discussed in the Introduction, is born.

What we want to achieve is "dynamic architecture"—architecture specifically aimed at agility and facilitating change. This applies to both aspects of architecture: content and process.

The first aspect of dynamic architecture is content—that is, architecture as a product. An architecture must be constructed so that changes in the architecture, to accommodate new and unexpected developments, can be implemented as quickly and as cheaply as possible. The architecture can then quickly support changes in the business processes.

The second aspect concerns the processes around architecture: How to deal with architecture within the organization. The process of development and maintenance of an architecture should be implemented as a dynamic process, thereby ensuring that the organization can make use of the architecture effectively and efficiently.

By the content of dynamic architecture, we mean such aspects as *N*-tier architecture, open standards, generic *application programming interfaces* (APIs), component-based development, and service-oriented architecture. These approaches are mostly aimed at the breaking down of IT support into autonomous building blocks that can be developed, maintained, and changed independently of each other. In this way, changes to parts of the provision of information can be carried out quickly because they are restricted to clearly defined components. This is the well-known "Lego principle."[2]

The process side of architecture is generally underexposed. The way in which architecture is employed within an organization, however, is *crucial* in achieving the agility required—and therefore the primary focus of this book is the process side of architecture.

The following are examples of architectural principles that result in an architecture (i.e., a product) that is explicitly designed to adapt itself to changing circumstances:

- Data must be registered and maintained in one location.
- Applications may retrieve data only from an authorized source.
- Clearly defined uncoupling points must be introduced between all main processes and information provision services.
- In IT systems, control and execution mechanisms must be implemented separately.
- Presentation of information, business logic, and registration of data must be implemented separately.
- Control is applied to the interfaces instead of the internal working of the systems (the "black box" approach).
- Standard interface and integration techniques will be used.

The critical success factor for working under architectural guidance, in the present dynamic time, lies in the way that architecture is employed within an organization. We present a way of using architecture that is focused on enabling change.

The following aspects are distinctive to this approach:

- *Multidisciplinary cooperation.* Architecture is a joint venture between the business and IT.

- *Just enough, just in time.* The trigger for developing architecture is a concrete business objective. The business objective determines both the focus and priority of architectural activities. The architectural team is kept small and, where necessary, expanded with employees from other departments.

- *Project-start architecture.* Development projects are guided and supported in their use of architecture by providing them with a project-start architecture.

- *Standards and templates.* Both the design of architecture and the development of IT solutions are accelerated by using standards and templates.

- *Strategies.* In addition to the standard way of complying with the architecture, a defensive and an offensive strategy have been developed, in which, by way of exception, a temporary IT solution is created that does not comply with the architectural guidelines. By introducing an explicit mechanism for deviation, the unavoidable incidental divergence from the architecture can be adequately managed and kept under control.

ENABLING CHANGE

As stated at the beginning of this chapter, the architecture must be capable of reacting to changing circumstances quickly and adequately. The architecture must enable change. The main problem in working under architectural guidance is not so much the architecture itself, but how the architecture is used. Exhibit 3.4 provides a model that shows the way to establish the position of an architecture within an organization.

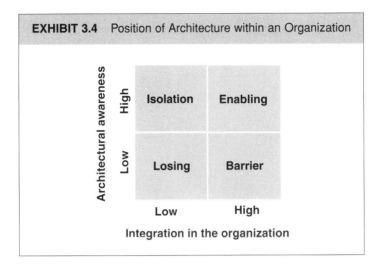

EXHIBIT 3.4 Position of Architecture within an Organization

The model is two dimensional. The first dimension is the level of architectural awareness: Does the organization possess a strategic and realistic vision and policy on IT and architecture? Is this policy an integral part of the overall policy for the organization? In organizations that score high on this scale, decision makers have a clear view of architecture and know what they want to achieve by using architecture. Being aware of architecture and being able to translate this into vision and policy is not enough, however. Policies need to be translated into action. The second dimension, therefore, is the level of integration of architecture within the organization: Are the architectural processes fully implemented and are enough resources allocated (people and money) to ensure that "working under architecture" is more than just a phrase and actually takes place within the organization?

Exhibit 3.5 illustrates the distinguishing characteristics of each quadrant. The quadrant, in which an organization best fits, reveals the potential of the organization to adequately react to developments in the market.

EXHIBIT 3.5   Distinguishing Characteristics of Each Quadrant

Isolation

- IT is experienced as being strategically important
- Business–IT alignment takes place frequently
- IT vision, strategy, policy, and choices are part of the business strategy
- Supported to a great extent by third parties, thus forming an unacceptable risk
- Architectural processes are not institutionalized within the organization
- IT is doing the right things
- IT is effective but lacks efficiency

Enabling

- IT is experienced as being strategically important
- Business–IT alignment takes place frequently
- IT vision, strategy, policy, and choices are part of the business strategy
- The organization is in control of the key competences
- The level of architecture is continually increased by riding on the wave of energy created by pursuing a business objective
- IT is doing the right things properly
- IT is both effective and efficient.

If an organization combines a high level of architectural awareness with a high level of architectural integration, then it will be found in the *enabling* quadrant. Organizations in this quadrant are able to utilize the full potential of IT. They have a clear vision of architecture and have already implemented this vision in the business change processes. Architecture has been institutionalized and has become an integral part of the functioning of the organization.

EXHIBIT 3.5 *(Continued)*	
Losing	**Barrier**
• IT is not perceived as being strategically important	• IT is not perceived as being strategically important
• Business–IT alignment does not take place	• Business–IT alignment does not take place
• No stated IT vision, strategy, policy, or choices	• IT vision, strategy, policy, and choices have been defined but are fragmented and lacking in purpose
• No resources, or insufficient resources, allocated to IT	• Sufficient, or more than sufficient, resources allocated to IT but the right things are still not being done
• IT is neither effective nor efficient	• The business ignores IT and shops for solutions elsewhere
	• IT is efficient but not effective

An organization in the *barrier* quadrant combines a low level of architectural awareness with a high level of architectural integration. Effectively, this means that the organization has appointed architects to design architecture, but that the impact of architecture on the organization is not fully understood and is, in fact, underestimated. The organization misses a clear vision on the importance of architecture. Architecture is seen as an IT issue and an efficiency tool for the IT department. The organization cannot make the essential link between architecture and attaining business objectives. Organizations in this quadrant run the risk of developing architecture for architecture's sake.

Organizations in the *isolation* quadrant combine a high level of architectural awareness with a low level of architectural integration. These organizations, up to and including top management, recognize the importance of architecture but the architecture processes are insufficiently embedded within the organization. The resources necessary to actually implement architecture within the organization have not been allocated. Management possesses a sound vision and policy of architecture, and everyone knows what should be done, but it just does not happen. Some organizations try to solve this problem by bringing in third-party expertise, but that solution offers only temporary relief. The organization needs to allocate sufficient resources to allow architectural awareness to permeate the very pores of the organization.

In the fourth quadrant, *losing*, we find organizations that combine a low level of architectural awareness with a low level of architectural integration. These organizations are not aware that IT is strategically important and that architecture plays an essential part in substantiating this strategic role. The organization is standing on the outside looking in; however, it does not know what it is looking at. Architecture is not even on the agenda. This is a very risky position—especially when competitors recognize the importance of IT and architecture.

During METAmorphosis 2000, the annual META group congress, the META group warned about what they called the "efficiency trap." An IT department (or service provider) is caught in the efficiency trap if the business does not trust it enough to discuss issues other than the efficiency of IT. The IT department will subsequently be judged only on efficiency and not on effectiveness. Once caught in this trap, it appears to be very difficult to get out. If we project the efficiency trap on our model in Exhibit 3.4, we would position it in the *barrier* quadrant. For that reason, it is recommended that the correct way to proceed from *losing* to *enabling* is through *isolation* and not through *barrier*.

The quadrant model can be used as an aid to determine the position of architecture within an organization. In the next chapter, we will discuss which improvements are linked to each of the quadrants.

QUICKLY ACHIEVING BUSINESS OBJECTIVES: DYA

Architecture has always been aimed at achieving coherence. To enable change, agility must be applied both to the architecture and to the way the architecture is used (i.e., the architectural processes). In the following chapter, we introduce Dynamic Architecture for modeling and development—DYA. Dynamic, in this context, stands for agility, while architecture stands for coherence. DYA is both a theoretical and a working model. It is an aid to implementing and improving architectural processes and covers the full range—from determining the business objectives to realizing IT solutions.

Notes

1. Design and implementation in the definition comprise the following activities for producing IT solutions: detailed design, selection, construction, implementation, and support and maintenance.

2. For more information on component thinking, see Butler Group, "Component-Based Development" (Butler Group, 1998); Han Van Der Zee, Paul Laagland, Bas Hafkenscheid, and Leonie Geersing, *Architectuur als Managementinstrument: Multi Client Study* [Architecture as Management Instrument: A Multiclient Study] (The Hague: Ten Hagen & Stam, 2000); and P.F. D'Souza and A.C. Wills, *Objects, Components and Frameworks with UML: The Catalysis Approach* (Reading, MA: Addison-Wesley, 1998). For information on the integration of applications, see D. S. Linthicum, *Enterprise Application Integration* (Reading, MA: Addison-Wesley, 1999); and T. Schadler, S.D. Woodring, C.S. Overby, and J. Walker, "Getting Apps to Work Together" (Forrester Research, Inc., June 1998).

CHAPTER 4

The DYA Model

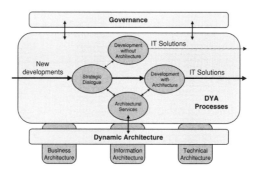

MAKING IT WORK

How can architecture be brought into play successfully? Which concrete measures can an organization take to ensure the continued optimum use of architecture? The answers to these questions have been combined into a model called *DYA*. This model is the result of bringing together the practical experience of IT development from many kinds of organizations. The DYA model provides both tangible, usable tools and allows for diversity in implementation. Diversity is needed because each organization differs—and what will work for one organization does not work for another. Each organization must be able to implement architecture in a way that suits best.

The DYA model gives a complete picture of working under architecture, a picture from which architects can select those parts of the model that are most useful to them. The full model or just a part of the model can be used, depending on the actual level of working under architecture within an organization.

TEN PRINCIPLES OF DYA

Before introducing the content and use of the model, ten principles—the precepts and presumptions of Dynamic Architecture—need to be presented:

1. *Architecture is strategic if IT is strategic.* IT is of strategic importance. Developments in IT can cause radical changes to both the business strategy of an organization and its business model. IT is decisive in attaining a competitive edge and provides the

---

conditions necessary for attracting and retaining customers. Architecture is, therefore, of strategic importance as well. It is indispensable in realizing the full potential of IT.

2. *Architecture must facilitate speed of change.* The present market climate gives organizations an increasingly shorter reaction time to adequately deal with external and internal developments. Speed of change has become a critical factor for success. Architecture should be an enabling factor in developing this speed of change.

3. *Communication between business and IT management is crucial.* Sound communication between business and IT management is a prerequisite to realizing the full strategic potential of IT. Business and IT strategy are a combined responsibility and must therefore be formulated by both disciplines.

4. *Business objectives govern the development of architecture.* The effort and expenditure needed for working under architecture can only be justified if architecture assists in achieving business objectives. Development of architecture must be driven by business objectives. Without this principle, there may soon be the rather vague situation of "architecture for architecture's sake." Architects should focus on achieving specific business objectives instead of focusing on the autonomous development of a companywide architecture.

5. *The level of architecture will be continually raised if architecture is aligned to important business changes.* Architectural investments have a good chance of being approved if they are both the result and an integral part of the investment necessary to attain an important business objective. This principle underlines the architecture's purposeful approach to achieving business objectives, and also emphasizes that without it convincing the business of the need to raise the level of architecture becomes nearly impossible.

6. *Architecture must be developed "just enough, just in time."* "Just-enough, just-in-time" development means that the various components of architecture will only be developed when it is clear how and for what purpose they will be used. In other words,

when it is clear that business objectives will be achieved with the architecture. The allocation of architectural resources varies with the dynamics and frequency of the business objectives being pursued: More demand for architecture means more architects, less demand means fewer architects.

7. *Working under architecture is supported by a theoretical and working model.* The inherent differences in business needs and strategies between organizations preclude a simple, unambiguous, step-by-step recipe for implementing working under architecture. Although these differences influence the way to employ architecture as a whole, there is a genuine need for concrete guidance in designing architecture to the needs of an organization. Working under architecture does not happen by itself, and it is advisable to implement it by following widely accepted theories and best practices. The DYA model provides both tangible, usable tools, and enough room for diversity in implementation. Architects can utilize the various parts of the model that are most suitable to them, and elaborate on these components to meet the specific needs of the organization.

8. *Transparent relationships must be defined.* By providing a clear insight into the relationships between the various architectural objects (processes, information, applications, etc.) and the various architectural levels (strategic, tactical, and operational) within an organization, it will become obvious where choices and agreements must be made. A clear insight into these relationships helps determine which domains of an architecture need further elaboration.

9. *Several development strategies are distinguished.* If time is limited, and there is a great deal of pressure to develop an IT solution for a specific business objective, an organization must be able to rely on alternative development strategies in which deliberate noncompliance to the architecture is allowed. The key factor in this principle is that, parallel to the development of a solution using one of these noncompliance strategies, an architecturally sound solution is recreated. In this way, incidental noncompliant developments become part of the standard way

of working and the risk of uncontrolled growth of noncompliant solutions will be reduced.

10. *Architectural principles and processes must be an integral part of the organization.* Without the willingness to embed the architectural principles and processes into an organization, the organization will never obtain an information function that adequately responds to its wishes and demands.

These principles make it clear that developing an architecture is not an autonomous process, but an integral part of the process to attain a specific business goal. We paraphrase this with the motto: "Just-enough, just-in-time architecture." Architecture is subservient to business objectives. This means that architecture should be on the agenda of business, not just on that of the IT department. To this end, communication between business and IT management occupies a central position in the DYA model. Agility is also an essential aspect of the model. The ten principles of DYA state the contours of the theoretical and working model that are detailed in the rest of the chapter.

DYA: A THEORETICAL AND WORKING MODEL

The DYA model consists of two parts: (1) a theoretical model and (2) a working model. The theoretical model combines the architectural concepts that make up DYA. The working model describes how the theoretical model can be implemented.

DYA as a Theoretical Model

The DYA theoretical model is shown in Exhibit 4.1. The outer circle represents the company as a whole; the inner circle represents IT. A company develops a vision, determines strategies, and formulates objectives with a strong emphasis on the interests of its stakeholders. The company's stakeholders in the exhibit are identified as its customers, partners, shareholders, and employees. All stakeholders try to defend their interests by placing demands on company policy, thus exerting their influence on the vision, strategy, and objectives of the company. For example, customers demand good service; partners want to rely on contractual agreements; shareholders demand a positive (financial) result; and employees demand a good salary and employee benefits. Business strategies and objectives should provide the answers to these demands for the present as well as the future.

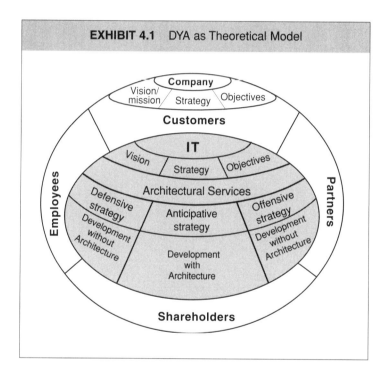

EXHIBIT 4.1   DYA as Theoretical Model

In addition to the influences exerted by the stakeholders, there is a mutual influence between business strategy and IT strategy. Business has always influenced IT because IT is intended to support the business. Changes in business strategy, therefore, always influence IT strategy, and IT must continue to be an enabling factor in carrying out business policies. But the influence is also the other way round. IT also influences business strategy. Developments, especially technological advances, in IT can be responsible for far-reaching changes in the business strategy. IT creates possibilities that were not considered before or were thought to be impossible. To gain a maximum of business value from these new possibilities, they must be incorporated into the business strategy. The increase in business potential, created by new possibilities, will also influence the stakeholders' demands and expectations.

For example, e-commerce can be used to increase the level of services offered to customers. Synergy can be achieved by linking the company's IT systems to those of its partners. Shareholders appreciate that the efficiency increase gained by the additional use of IT has a direct (positive!) effect on the company's results. Enterprising, technologically savvy employees gladly seize the opportunity to work at home as a result of using the bandwidth offered by modern network technology.

In short, company strategy, the stakeholders' demands, and IT strategy influence each other.

The inner circle in Exhibit 4.1 represents the company's IT facility. The exhibit shows that three possible strategies have been defined:

1. The anticipatory strategy
2. The defensive strategy
3. The offensive strategy

The difference between these three strategies underlines the principle that, in addition to the standard way of working under architecture (the anticipatory strategy), there must be room for deliberate noncompliance (the defensive and offensive strategies).

The anticipatory strategy aims at providing solutions with a high anticipatory capacity. This means that the provision of information is flexible and changeable and, for that reason, able to react swiftly to impulses from the environment. This strategy is based firmly on the concepts of Dynamic Architecture. The IT solutions developed with this strategy are all said to be developed "under architecture"—that is, development with architecture.

Even a fully implemented Dynamic Architecture cannot prevent the sudden threats and opportunities that confront an organization where the time available to provide an adequate solution is insufficient. In real life, situations will always arise where, driven by the urgency of the situation, an organization feels obliged to deviate from the architecture on certain specific points. This can have several different reasons:

- The architectural principles have not been fully implemented so that the ability to change cannot be utilized.

- The present legacy situation makes compliance with architecture difficult.

- The necessary resources are not available.

- The pressure to provide a quick solution is so great that only the present situation is relevant, and there is no time to consider the future or other developments within the organization.

- The organization wishes to make use of a completely new IT development and the architecture is just not ready to accommodate it.

It is important to develop alternate strategies to deal with these kinds of situations and to incorporate them into the organization's normal way of working. These alternate strategies in the DYA model are the *defensive strategy* and the *offensive strategy*. The defensive strategy contends with eventualities that suddenly threaten the continuance of the organization, whereas the offensive strategy deals with business opportunities that require an immediate response from the organization. We describe development using the defensive or offensive strategy as "development without architecture" to indicate that this development does not need to comply with the standard architecture. By additionally creating a specific mechanism within defensive and offensive strategies to replace the noncompliant solutions with structural, compliant solutions, the organization can ensure that temporary developments are eventually replaced by permanent ones.

DYA as Working Model

A theoretical model has true value when it can be used in everyday practice. This is why the theoretical model has been complemented with a working model. The working model allows the theoretical model to be brought into practice. The DYA working model consists of three main processes: (1) the Strategic Dialogue, (2) Architectural Services, and (3) Development with(out) Architecture.[1]

The Strategic Dialogue determines which business objectives will be pursued—and ensures that the right things are done at the right time. This dialogue defines a business objective in a business case and then elaborates the objective as a concrete project proposal. This process is a collaboration of business and IT management who together determine which business objectives should be pursued. Multidisciplinary teams, working closely together, next further detail these objectives in business cases. A business case describes how an objective can be reached, what this entails for the organization, and what the financial consequences will be in terms of investment, annual costs, and returns. If the result of a business case is positive, a concrete project proposal is formulated.

Architectural Services is the process in which architectures are developed and made available to business case teams and project teams. It is a cyclical process in which the level of architecture is continually being raised. Architectural Services facilitates both the Strategic Dialogue and the Development with Architecture processes. The trigger for Architectural Services is always a concrete business case that needs further elaboration. Architectural Services ensures that things are done correctly.

Development with(out) Architecture achieves concrete business objectives within the desired time frame, with the desired level of quality, and with acceptable costs.

Development *with* Architecture is the standard and every project team following this strategy is furnished with the project-start architecture. The general architectural rules, guidelines, and models are "translated" into a project-start architecture that meets the specific problems confronting the project. The project-start architecture describes the concrete standards, norms, and guidelines to be used by the project. Development decisions, of relevance to more than the one project, are also detailed in the project-start architecture. The project-start architecture is drawn up by architects in close consultation with the project team.

Under special circumstances, for example, if an extremely urgent situation arises and time is limited, a deliberate choice can be made to develop a noncompliant solution. In this case, the Development *without* Architecture process is used. Certain aspects of architecture are temporarily ignored in a controlled and orderly fashion. *Controlled and orderly* as measures are taken to ensure that the solution provided by the Development without Architecture process eventually are brought under architecture by creating a permanent, structural solution for the problem. These measures are detailed in a "Management Letter." The Management Letter can be seen as a contract between the business manager, the project manager, and the architect that explicitly defines the temporary nature of an IT solution and contains the agreed-upon way in which money (and other resources), functionality, and quality must be sacrificed to achieve the deadline set by the defensive or offensive strategy. The Management Letter also states the course of action that has been agreed upon to achieve the structural solution, as required by the anticipatory strategy, and when this course of action will be implemented. Development with(out) Architecture ensures that the correct things are done correctly.

In the working model, the anticipatory strategy is, therefore, furnished by the Development with Architecture process, while the defensive and offensive strategies are accomplished by the Development without Architecture process. The choice of which strategy to use for which objective is made in the Strategic Dialogue process. Strategic Dialogue provides a mechanism for the mutual influencing and fine-tuning of business strategy and IT strategy and provides a road map for the other processes. The three processes of Strategic Dialogue, Architectural Services, and Development with(out) Architecture are described in detail in Chapters 5, 6, and 7.

Architecture should provide guidance to the design and realization of processes, organizational structures, information systems, and technical infrastructures for an organization. Architecture is, in this sense, a management tool that can be used to direct and control IT developments. Working under architecture itself also needs direction and management to function effectively. It is not enough for an organization to decide that, from now on, it is going to work under architectural guidance. Once the decision has been made, the organization needs to monitor that working under architecture actually happens and that the desired results are achieved. The final responsibility for this lies with top management. The term that we use for directing and controlling working under architecture is *governance*. Governance is the last component of the model and is described in detail in Chapter 8.

The relationships between the various components of the working model are illustrated in Exhibit 4.2. Its three main processes—Strategic Dialogue, Architectural Services, and Development with(out) Archi-

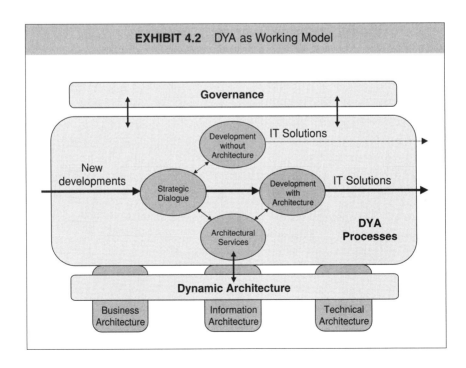

EXHIBIT 4.2 DYA as Working Model

tecture—have a cyclical character. The activities within the processes are, in fact, being performed continually, and they influence each other continually. At any given moment, various cycles can be performed simultaneously. While some projects are busy ensuring that business objectives determined by a previous cycle of the Strategic Dialogue are realized as soon as possible, a new cycle of the Strategic Dialogue has already been started, in which new opportunities can be identified that in turn lead to new business objectives, new business cases, and new project proposals.

THE MODEL AND THE PRINCIPLES

The DYA model provides substance to the 10 principles discussed in this chapter:

1. *Architecture is strategic if IT is strategic.* This principle is reflected in the model in that the final responsibility for architecture lies explicitly with top management.
2. *Architecture must facilitate speed of change.* This principle is implemented in the model by working in multidisciplinary teams and by providing a project with a project-start architecture. Models constructed during the definition of a business case are made available to a project in the project-start architecture, thereby providing the project with a flying start.
3. *Communication between business and IT management is crucial.* Business and IT management collaborate in the Strategic Dialogue to decide on which business objects to pursue.
4. *Business objectives govern the development of architecture.* Development of an architecture always takes place to achieve a concrete business objective. The Architectural Services process is driven by the Strategic Dialogue process that determines the business objectives.
5. *The level of architecture will be continually raised if architecture is aligned to important business changes.* The architectural processes are intended to enable the business change processes of an

organization. This automatically ensures that architectural investments become an integral part of the business investments necessary to achieve concrete business objectives.

6. *Architecture must be developed "just enough, just in time."* Concrete guidelines for implementing the "just-enough, just-in-time" principle are discussed in full in Chapter 6, Architectural Services. We shall see that one of the ways in which this principle manifests itself is the way in which the architectural team is manned: There is a small, fixed team of architects that, depending on the workload, can be temporarily increased by employees from the line organization. Just enough, just in time will also be ensured by involving architects from the outset— that is, during the definition of business cases. The ability to recognize the different levels of abstraction within architecture is helpful in developing just-enough, just-in-time architecture.

7. *Working under architecture is supported by a theoretical and working model.* A model has been developed for working under architecture that contains all of the important elements of architecture: the dynamic architecture itself, the three main processes of architecture, and the governance of architecture.

8. *Transparent relationships must be defined.* An architectural framework is an important tool for an architect and is discussed in detail in Chapter 6. The architectural framework provides clear insight into the relationships in an organization.

9. *Several development strategies are distinguished.* This principle is translated directly into the three development strategies: (1) the anticipatory strategy for working under architecture and (2) the defensive and (3) offensive strategies, in which certain aspects of architecture are temporarily ignored.

10. *Architectural principles and processes must be an integral part of the organization.* The focus of the model lies on architecture as a *process*, encompassing the whole trajectory from determining business objectives to creating IT solutions. Moreover, the model stresses the importance of a strong commitment from top management.

HOW TO USE THE MODEL

A model is nice to have—yet what can an organization do with it in everyday life? It has already been established that the DYA model can be used by an organization to implement or improve architectural processes. Before we begin implementing or improving the architectural process, we need to clarify what the organization actually wants to achieve—that is, to answer this question: What is the prime reason for wanting to raise the level of architecture? Possible reasons include:

- The organization wants to offer its products and services via new channels such as the Internet.
- The time-to-market for new products and services needs to be shortened.
- The organization wants to outsource the development of IT systems.
- The maintenance and support costs of IT systems must be reduced.
- The IT budget must be used more effectively and efficiently.
- The front-office and back-office processes need better alignment.

All of the above reasons demand working under architecture to achieve and retain the necessary coherence.

Once the objectives are clear, we can examine where improvements are necessary in working under architecture. With this information we can select those elements of the model that add the most value to the organization. The quadrant model introduced in Chapter 3, and shown again in Exhibit 4.3, is a helpful tool in this process. As we have already seen, this model has two dimensions that together determine the relative position of architecture within an organization: the level of architectural awareness and the level of integration of architecture within the organization.

Depending on where the organization is situated in the quadrant model, the emphasis for improvement is placed on different elements of DYA.

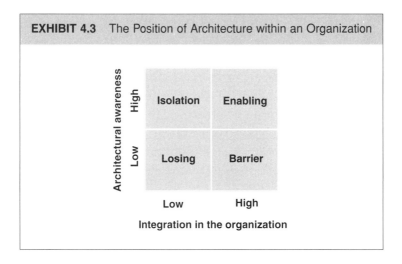

EXHIBIT 4.3 The Position of Architecture within an Organization

An organization will not escape this quadrant unless architecture

Losing

Organizations in the *losing quadrant* have a low level of awareness and integration. Working under architecture does not play a significant role in these organizations. Here and there, within the organization, some activities related to architecture may exist. However, they are mostly *ad hoc* and usually initiated by an "enlightened" employee. Architectural policy is nonexistent, and the role of "architect" is not even recognized. In short, architecture is not on the agenda.

An organization will not escape this quadrant unless architecture gets on the agenda of top management. The aspiring architect should begin by creating awareness, starting with his IT management. This is the right moment to bring the DYA concept to the attention of IT management. The tenuous balance between speed and cohesion can be used to illustrate why architecture is important and which issues it can address. Fear of creating an "ivory tower" can be defused by explaining the concept of Dynamic Architecture. Once IT management is convinced, a concerted effort can be planned to convince business management of the need for architecture.

Barrier

Organizations in the *barrier quadrant* have implemented architectural processes in their IT departments—however, architectural awareness is restricted to *just* the IT department. Business management is not involved; and how the IT departments conduct their own affairs is of no interest to them. In this situation, several employees have been designated to the role of architect and share the responsibility of delivering "architecture." Their activities, however, are fragmented, isolated, and specific to a particular department, domain, or project, and they create architecture that deals only with their specific challenges and problems.

In order to progress from this quadrant, awareness of architecture must be raised from the individual domain, usually created with an IT-centric view, to a level that encompasses the whole organization. The first priority, in spreading architectural awareness, is to involve the business. At this stage, it is important to present architecture as an enabler instead of a hindrance. The differences between the defensive/offensive strategies and the anticipatory strategy should be stressed, and emphasis should be placed on the purposeful approach in achieving business objectives of the architectural processes.

The various initiatives to introduce architecture must be coordinated to achieve greater cohesion between the initiatives. To help structure the initiatives, we will introduce the Architectural Framework in Chapter 6. Using this framework, the various initiatives fall into place and their mutual relationships become clear.

Finally, business management should recognize that they are restricting business development if they consider IT as a purely supportive process instead of a source of new possibilities. It is, therefore, essential that a form of Strategic Dialogue is initiated and that multidisciplinary business teams are installed—points that will be elaborated in Chapter 5.

Isolation

In the *isolation quadrant,* an organization, up to and including top management, recognizes the importance of architecture. Nevertheless, architectural processes are insufficiently embedded within the organization. Even though the Strategic Dialogue is a "well-oiled," productive process, the organization is not equipped to achieve the vision and plans that it produced.

To progress from this quadrant, all constructive ideas about architecture need to be embedded into the organization. One characteristic of an organization in this quadrant is that there are plenty of ideas about architecture on paper. However, the organization's management does not know where to begin implementing these ideas. Organizations in this quadrant are helped by the sense of purpose behind the DYA model. The architectural process as a whole needs to be transformed from an isolated, autonomous process into a facilitating process. Projects must also be convinced to actually start working under architecture. The project-start architecture can be a good tool in accomplishing this major step.

Enabling

Organizations in the *enabling quadrant* have attained an adequate level of awareness and integration. In this quadrant, organizations are properly equipped to work on continued improvement and innovation. The processes of Strategic Dialogue, Architectural Services, and Development with(out) Architecture have been implemented in full. All that needs to be done is to keep monitoring these processes and, where necessary, carry out improvements.

Depending on where the organization is situated in the quadrant model, the emphasis for improvement is placed on different elements of DYA, which is summarized in Exhibit 4.4.

FILLING IN THE MODEL

Now that the components and usage of the DYA model have been described, it is time to provide more detail and make some of the ideas presented so far more concrete.

EXHIBIT 4.4	Quadrant Model and DYA Aspects

Quadrant	Emphasis on
Losing	Create awareness with IT management: Bring the importance of architecture to the attention of IT management and explain the DYA concept.
Barrier	Involve the business: Consider the defensive/offensive strategy and the purposeful character of architecture.
	Bring structure and cohesion into the various architecture initiatives using the architectural framework.
	Initiate communication between business and IT management by implementing the Strategic Dialogue and multidisciplinary business case teams.
Isolation	Integrate architecture: Implement Architectural Services as a facilitating process.
	Introduce a project-start architecture
Enabling	Monitor the Strategic Dialogue, Architectural Services, and Development with(out) Architecture as a continuous process of innovation and improvement.

In the following chapters, we further discuss the main processes of the DYA model. Strategic Dialogue, Architectural Services, and Development with(out) Architecture each have a chapter. We will describe (and advise on) the activities, products, and people that make up these processes. The subject of Governance is covered in Chapter 8.

In the course of the following chapters, we will identify the parts of the DYA model that help avoid the traps, identified in Chapter 2, into which traditional methods often fall:

- Traditionally, architecture is provided by a project with a planning horizon of a year or more. DYA uses the cyclic Architectural Services process, which continuously provides just-enough, just-in-time architecture.

- In using the Strategic Dialogue, tools are provided to bridge the gap between the business and IT.

- As opposed to developing an architecture for the entire organization in one go, DYA propagates a just-enough, just-in-time approach that develops architectures per domain as and when needed.

- As opposed to an autonomous activity for the IT department that does not consider the rest of the organization, DYA aids the implementation of an architectural process that is fully integrated into the business change process of the organization.

- Simply ignoring the architectural process altogether is made more difficult for projects by explicitly offering the possibility of creating a temporary solution that does not comply with the architecture.

Note

1. The bracketed "out" signifies that, in addition to development with architecture (the anticipatory strategy), there is room for incidentally developing noncompliant solutions without architecture (the defensive or offensive strategy).

CHAPTER 5

Strategic Dialogue

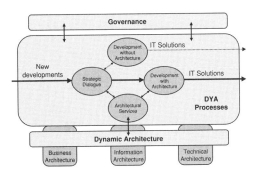

CRISIS AT WWW-TELEBEL

The project team for WWW-TeleBel, the new Internet portal for TeleBel customers, is facing a crisis. Its leader, Tom Alberts, is pacing the corridor and looking flushed. Project team members are spending more time philosophizing about how to continue the project rather than drawing up a functional design. The project is running behind schedule.

Everything seems to be going wrong. It started at the beginning of the week with a message from the administrator of the billing system stating that the required interface will be delivered three months later than planned. The reason is a change of priorities. Rumour has it that the company is considering purchasing a new billing system and would prefer not to invest any more in the existing system. In addition, External Communication complained that the webpages designed by the project team did not meet the corporate style requirements. The look and feel are not right—and neither is the design of the login and navigation procedures. To top it all, higher management issued a statement this morning that IT costs are too high again and cuts would be made in certain projects. Next month, a large-scale inventory will be made of all projects, and the results will be used to decide which projects continue and which cease. Until that time, projects should not incur any costs. So, for the moment, Alberts' team can forget about hiring two Internet specialists.

Alberts is muttering to himself as he walks back and forth in the corridor. "It is always the same in this company," he tells himself. "Agreements are not worth the paper they are written on, everybody interferes in everything, and funds can be cut at any time. How can you ever get a project properly finished?"

STRATEGIC DIALOGUE: DOING THE RIGHT THINGS

Things are not running well at TeleBel. Priorities change at the drop of a hat. Projects are stopped halfway through because funds run out. Projects suddenly face unpleasant, conflicting developments within the organization. TeleBel clearly needs to focus its IT development with clearly defined objectives—and then link its IT projects to these objectives—so that it is easy to see why each project is carried out and what its results will be.

The first key process in the DYA model—Strategic Dialogue—addresses these issues. The Strategic Dialogue process ensures that the organization does the right things. It makes IT development goal-oriented.

Within the Strategic Dialogue, there are two distinct subprocesses. In the first subprocess, *determining business cases*, IT and business management determine together which business objectives the organization should pursue. In the second subprocess, *elaborating business cases*, the selected business objectives are described in greater detail to create business cases. A business case describes how an objective can be achieved, that is, when, in what way, at what cost, and how the organization will benefit. Projects are only started on the basis of an accepted business case for a concrete business objective formulated by the organization.

The Strategic Dialogue not only governs which IT developments occur. It also determines the reference framework for all efforts in the field of architecture. The Strategic Dialogue provides the trigger for setting up architectures. When it is decided to describe a business case in greater detail, the architects act to provide the necessary architectural principles and models. Thus, setting up an architecture is also done in a goal-orientated way and the phenomenon of "architecture for the sake of the architecture" is not given a chance.

DETERMINING BUSINESS CASES

The first step in the Strategic Dialogue is to determine the business objectives of the organization—and this is done by business and IT managers together. Because developments in IT happen fast and have such an influence on business strategy, it is no longer possible for separation in determining objectives and strategy, where the business side of the organization determines business objectives and then has the IT side add the accompanying IT strategy. The market and IT influence each other too much. Only when there is an integral approach to the market and IT can the organization make full use of all opportunities and counter any threats such as those evolving from e-business. In the case of e-business, being successful means ensuring that all specializations, both in the field of business and IT, come together at the right time. The architect plays an advisory role in this crucial coming together. It is the architect's task to follow developments in the economic sector, business and IT, and to convert these into opportunities for the organization itself.

Determining the business objectives starts at the top management level. That is where objectives for the organization as a whole are established. These objectives are then converted by middle management— at all levels, communication between business and IT is essential—into concrete objectives for the individual units. This creates a hierarchy of objectives. Furthermore, determining business objectives requires an assessment of developments not only in the market and in society but also in the field of IT, as well as the resulting opportunities that it makes possible.

The following three steps need to be taken:

Step 1. Identify possible business objectives

Step 2. Identify IT enablers for the organization

Step 3. Select business objectives to be elaborated into business cases

Identifying Possible Business Objectives

The first step is for business and IT to jointly list possible business objectives. This differs from what is common in many organizations, where the IT department assesses the annual plans for the business and bases its policies on it accordingly. Because business and IT discuss business objectives together, there is greater mutual understanding, clarity, support, and creativity.

Identifying IT Enablers for the Organization

To determine the relevance of IT developments in achieving the business objectives—and to specify these objectives in greater detail—another list must be drawn up—of potentially relevant IT developments. Examples include Internet technology, Computer Telephony Integration (CTI), and data warehousing.[1] This does not merely concern technical aspects but also issues such as supplier policies, the degree to which developments are accepted by the economic sector, and (expected) social acceptance.

The more specific the business objectives can be phrased, the greater the chance of successfully achieving them. The well-known rule of always formulating objectives in a SMART way, applies here too:

Specific. The objective must be described in precise, specific terms.

Measurable. It must be possible to determine when the objective has been achieved.

Acceptable. The organization must be willing to work on the objective.

Realistic. It must be possible to achieve the objective.

Timebound. A time must be set when the objective is to be achieved.

Using these simple guidelines has proven to contribute to the quality of the formulated objectives.

When the lists of business objectives and IT developments are complete, the two are placed side by side to determine the relevance of different IT developments to the desired business objectives. IT developments that contribute most to business objectives constitute the *IT enablers* for the organization.

A very effective and interactive way to quickly arrive at a selection of business objectives, a selection that can be supported by top management, is through what is called the *IT enabling session*. An IT-enabling session consists of one or more workshops in which a number of steps are taken that eventually lead to a priority list of business objectives, a priority list of relevant IT trends (the IT enablers), and a selection of business objectives that need to be further specified into business cases.

To identify the IT enablers, the IT trend/business objective model shown in Exhibit 5.1 serves as an aid. The model can be used to determine the relevance of specific IT trends for specific business objectives in a relatively short span of time—and established IT practices can also be included in this model to determine their relevancy. The model works as follows. For each business objective, a quadrant model is completed. The example in Exhibit 5.1 concerns the business objective of *increasing customer service* by longer opening hours and shorter response times. The model shows two dimensions: the effort that is required to adapt an IT trend to an organization and the expected results of the IT trend for that organization.

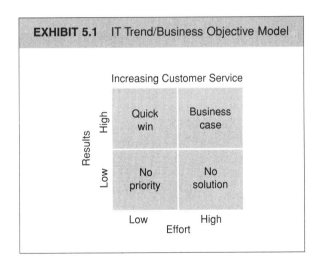

All IT trends are positioned in the model for each business objective. During an enabling session, participants discuss each trend and determine its importance for the business objective concerned. When agreement has been reached, a card with the name of the trend is placed in the quadrant. As shown in Exhibit 5.2, a weight factor is given to the quadrants that indicates the relevance of the trend for the business objective.

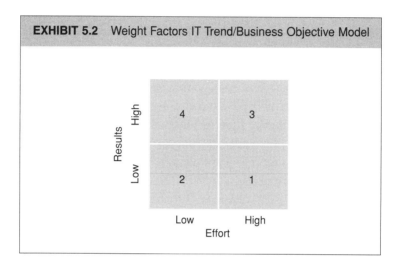

EXHIBIT 5.2   Weight Factors IT Trend/Business Objective Model

Participants proceed in this way until they have dealt with every trend in the context of that particular business objective. When all trends have been classified on the board, it can be seen at a glance which trends are important for a particular business objective.

The participants do the same for the remaining business objectives. Then, by adding up the scores of each IT trend for the various business objectives, as is shown in Exhibit 5.3, the result indicates the total importance of an IT trend for the organization (across the business objectives). An IT trend with a high score contributes to a large extent to the business objectives as a whole and, therefore, appears to be a good candidate for being labelled as an IT enabler. These potential IT enablers can then be investigated in greater detail.

On each line we can see the importance of the IT trends for the various business objectives. In the columns, we can see which IT trends are relevant for each business objective.

Business Objective IT Trend	Increasing Customer Service	Invoicing Over the Internet	Shorter Time-to-Market	Reduce Debtors Level	Total
EXHIBIT 5.3 IT Trends versus Business Objectives					
Internet technology	4	4	2	2	12
Smart cards	1	1	1	3	6
Electronic data exchange	1	3	2	4	10
Packages	2	1	2	1	6
Data warehousing	3	1	1	3	8
Call centers and CTI	4	3	2	1	10
Imaging	2	1	1	2	6
Message broker	1	3	1	4	9
Component-based development	1	3	4	2	10
DSDM	1	3	4	1	9
WAP	2	1	1	1	5

Selecting Business Objectives to Be Elaborated into Business Cases

On the basis of the insights obtained, the business objectives are listed by priority and then it is decided which will be elaborated into business cases. This includes indicating which IT trends are relevant to the business cases. Each business objective destined to become a business case is assigned to a particular person, preferably a decision maker. This person is responsible for the definition of the business case and for providing the results of this process to the same group that initially decided to create the business case. In addition, one person is made responsible for all business cases that are selected from the business objectives list. This *project portfolio management* is necessary to safeguard coherence and consistency—and is discussed in more detail in Chapter 8, Governance.

Determining current business objectives is not a one-of process. Both business and IT management need to be alert for new opportunities and threats. Therefore, it is wise to place the topic of "new opportunities" permanently on the agenda of management meetings. The interval should be, at least, every other week and not longer than one month because, in that case, the organization runs the risk of being too slow in responding to external developments. An alternative is to set up a procedure that enables the organization to discuss new opportunities at any given moment. A new opportunity, spotted by someone in the organization, then triggers a prompt meeting of the strategy team (or whatever name this formal or informal body has in the organization). Ideally, there should even be a set time for assessing new opportunities, such as every Friday from 8 A.M. to 9 A.M.

The final result of the subprocess of determining business cases is a strategic document containing prioritized business objectives, including motivation, prioritized IT enablers, including motivation, and a list of business cases to be elaborated, including prior conditions such as maximum duration, maximum cost, or minimum benefits.

The final result forms the *first level of approval*. On the basis of this first level of approval, it is decided which ideas are to be elaborated into business cases and which ideas should be abandoned.

As we will see in the next section, elaboration of business cases leads to concrete project proposals that are, in turn, put before top management for approval again. This constitutes the *second level of approval*. The second level of approval, therefore, concerns the decision to actually carry out a project.

ELABORATING BUSINESS CASES

The second subprocess in the Strategic Dialogue consists of elaborating selected business cases. Again, communication between business and IT plays a key role. Elaborating a business case means completing the following steps:

Step 1. Outlining an overall solution.

Step 2. Carrying out impact analyses.

Step 3. Detailing the financial basis.

Step 4. Drawing up a project proposal.

To complete these steps, a business case team is set up. This multidisciplinary team includes a person who is responsible for business, such as a product manager, employees from the line organization, one or more architects, information analysts, system experts, and a technical specialist. The team is led by the person responsible for the business.

The aim of having a multidisciplinary team is to achieve greater speed and effectiveness in the development process. As the group process is experienced by the team as a whole, its members acquire mutual understanding and broad support for the chosen solution. In addition, the process is accelerated because all perspectives are dealt with simultaneously, and the results are based on the actual situation. It is less likely that the team turns into a direction that leads nowhere.

IT employees are also involved in the business case, minimizing the risk of misunderstandings during the realization of IT systems that might be the result of the decision-making process on the elaborated business cases. Moreover, developers have a better understanding of the context in which they work from the perspective of the business and of the architecture.

In the business case, the following seven issues are defined in greater detail with regard to achieving the business objective (such as putting a new product on the market):

- *Objective*—This is where aim, background, direction of solution, and success factors of the business objective are dealt with.

- *Marketing*—In the case of a new product or a new service, this describes the intended market, the target audience, the product or the service itself, and any environmental factors that play a role.

- *Conditional Aspect*—These primarily include the legal and security aspects that need to be taken into account.

- *Implementation*—Which employees are affected by the business objective and, in what way; is there a need for new workplaces; are new resources required; how do business processes change, what changes occur in the registration of data; and, finally, do any business rules need to be changed?

- *Control*—How have responsibilities been assigned, what does the business objective's life cycle look like, and what management information should be delivered?

- *Financial Analysis*—What expenses will be involved in achieving the business objective and what will be the benefits?

- *Planning*—When will the business objective be achieved?

Outlining an Overall Solution

The first step in elaborating a business case is outlining the general direction in seeking the solution. During the course of a number of workshops, the business case team determines the business requirements, what the desired processes should look like, and what this means in overall terms for the information requirements. A useful approach here is that of TIPD (Technique for Interactive Process Design), which enables fast process modeling. (TIPD is discussed in Appendix A.)

During this phase, the architects supply the architectures (i.e., principles and models) that indicate the direction of the solution. In organizations where no architecture exists, this will be set up in the Architectural Services process. Here, the architects limit themselves to the architectural aspects that are relevant for the business case.

This is also the phase in which the issues of objective, marketing, and conditional aspects regarding the business objective are dealt with.

Carrying Out Impact Analyses

Impact analyses are carried out as soon as the overall solution has been outlined. This means looking at relevant subareas to assess the gap between solution and current situation and how this gap can be bridged. The architects provide the models—for both the existing situation and the desired situation. This phase also includes elaborations of implementation, control, and planning issues.

To carry out the impact analyses, a number of standard questions must be asked about each subarea. These are specifications of the main question: What needs to change? The template shown in Exhibit 5.4 can be used for this purpose. The dotted line represents the title of the respective column (business objectives, products/services, etc.).

In principle, the changes proposed in the impact analyses will comply with the architecture's requirements. It is possible, however, that changing situations or new insights will make adjustments to the architecture necessary. In that case, the impact of these changes to the architecture as a whole will be assessed. This is followed by an investigation into what these changes mean for projects that are already running.

For example, an organization wants to set up a front office to meet a number of aims that it has formulated in the field of customer orientation. This front office's staff must have access to all back-office applications and must be able to give overall discounts and test the creditworthiness of clients at group level. This set of demands may lead

EXHIBIT 5.4 Impact Analysis Template

	Business Objectives	Products / Services	Process	Organization	Data	Application	Platform	Network	Middleware
Which…is/are relevant?									
Which…can remain unchanged?									
Which…must be abolished?									
Which…must be changed?									
Which…must be added?									
What do the changed and new…look like?									
What must be done to achieve this?									

to standards in the field of interfacing, authorizations, unique key coding, and real-time processing demands. This can have consequences for other projects. These consequences should be defined clearly and be included in decision making.

Detailing the Financial Basis

When it is clear what is needed to achieve the desired business objective, a detailed financial basis is created. Indeed, in this phase, the financial section of the business case is written. This should indicate the costs and benefits, and whether the business case has a positive outcome. A business case is positive when the necessary investments for the business case yield the desired results for the organization. Ways to measure their success include determining the *returns on investments* (ROI) or the *net present value of investments* (NPV) and to establish whether these exceed a level previously agreed by the organization. Another approach, to accept or refuse a business case, is the method of *Information Economics* (IE). This method does not merely look at financial variables. It also looks at issues such as strategic need and risks. (Information Economics is discussed in Appendix B.)

Drawing up a Project Proposal

If the business case is not positive, no project proposal is formulated and the fate of the business case is turned over to top management, who will decide what happens next.

If the result is positive, the insights gained can be translated into a project proposal that includes, at least, the following issues: definition of the task; project organization; approach, products, and planning; handover, acceptance, implementation, and follow-up; resources; and finally, management aspects. A business case may lead to several projects, including rapid achievement of objectives parallel to a structural solution, in combination with a technical infrastructure project.

Project proposals are submitted to decision-making management, which decides whether or not to accept the proposals. This is where projects receive the classification of anticipative, defensive, or offensive, according to the development strategy used to carry out the projects. The standard classification is anticipative. Only if it becomes apparent, at some stage during the elaboration of the business case, that too little time exists to achieve the business objective under architecture, is the classification changed to offensive or defensive strategy. (In Chapter 7, Development with(out) Architecture, we will see what this actually means for the development route.)

Formulating a business case is sometimes regarded as a more or less bureaucratic hurdle that needs to be taken before the real work in the project can start. However, this step includes nothing that is unnecessary for achieving the business objective. If no business case is created, the activities described are often done implicitly, or if and when certain issues arise during the project. Practice has taught us that carrying out a business case explicitly is a much more efficient and effective method of operating. The main reason is that subsequent project activities can be targeted much more clearly. After all, the objective, the area of application, the assignment of responsibilities, the scope of the solution, the urgency, the effects of the solution, the time span, support, and standards and norms are clearly defined at the moment when the execution of the project starts. This also enables much better resource planning for the project.

Architects play an important role in the elaboration of business cases. They ensure that the right enterprise architectures are available at the right time. In this way, they not only support the business case team. They also are present at an early stage to steer the final solution in the right direction. This is much more effective than correcting afterward. Enterprise architecture is then soundly embedded in the organization's change process. The way in which architects fulfill their role is discussed in Chapter 6, Architectural Services. There we will also see that architects have a powerful tool at their disposal in the form of an enterprise architecture framework.

Exhibit 5.5 shows a diagram of the process of making a business case.

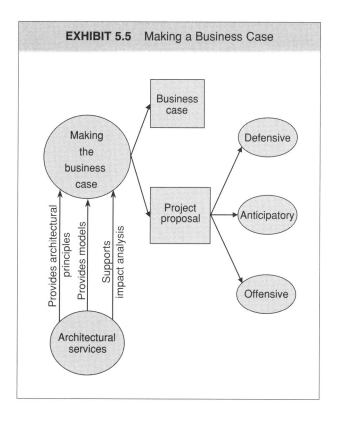

EXHIBIT 5.5   Making a Business Case

The subprocess of detailing the business case has two final products: (1) a business case and (2) a project proposal. At the end of this chapter, the business case for WWW-TeleBel is given as an example.

STRATEGIC DIALOGUE: COHERENCE AND AGILITY

The Strategic Dialogue constitutes the baseline for all enterprise architecture and IT development activities. This is where the decisions are taken regarding the focus of enterprise architecture and IT development. A well-organized Strategic Dialogue helps the organization to achieve coherence and agility.

One way to create coherence is by letting business and IT management cooperate in determining business objectives and by having multidisciplinary business case teams. As a result of this cooperation, business and IT developments are looked at and dealt with more in terms of their interrelationship. Using two levels of approval also contributes to achieving coherence: Project proposals for IT development are not assessed in isolation, but are compared against the organization's policy as a whole. Finally, the fact that architects are involved in the development of plans at an early stage also results in projects that fit better into the overall structure.

Agility also benefits from the multidisciplinary character of the business case teams. Combining knowledge and experience from different fields makes work more goal-oriented. In addition, the fact that architecture development takes place against the background of business objectives forces architects to stay alert and not lose themselves in enterprise architectures that have little or no relationship to reality.

INTERMEZZO: THE BUSINESS CASE FOR WWW-TELEBEL

Objective

Aim

WWW-TeleBel's purpose is to attract customers by offering consumers and small businesses the option of using the Internet and their personal computer to check the status of their telephone bill at any time.

Background

The idea for WWW-TeleBel emerged from existing customer requests. The growing popularity of the Internet and mobile telephony has caused a considerable increase in telephone fees, creating a need for consumers and small businesses to monitor their telephone usage more actively. Quarterly statements are no longer regarded as adequate. By making the current status of their accounts accessible over the Internet, this need would be met.

In addition, WWW-TeleBel offers added value by making the usage data available electronically. Customers can process this data administratively (e.g., paying their bill) and for analysis (e.g., for setting limits on usage).

Opening a new communication channel with the client by using the Internet provides the opportunity for additional benefits in the future by gradually introducing additional services and communication facilities.

Solution

To show current account data, use is made of a link with the existing billing systems. These existing systems compile the necessary data, with a new module processing it in such a way that it can be shown in standard web browsers.

For the Internet part, use is made of the existing Internet infrastructure, which was set up in order to be able to provide product information (electronic catalogue).

Success Factors

WWW-TeleBel will only be unique for about three months. Other telecommunication companies will follow suit, and the service becomes a commodity. From that moment, the distinguishing factor will be the innovative character of the introduction and implementation of new services offered to the user on this recently opened communication channel. Possibilities include the layout of data according to the client's specification (e.g., personalization of the webpage) or offering analytical programs for usage data (e.g., what-if scenarios). Agility and perpetual innovation are clear success factors for WWW-TeleBel. A dedicated product manager will, therefore, have to be appointed at WWW-TeleBel.

WWW-TeleBel will make a greater demand on Customer Service. Customer Service should be prepared for this. Bad service is lethal for WWW-TeleBel.

WWW-TeleBel's only chance of success is if all services used by the customer are included in the Internet bill. WWW-TeleBel must provide an overview of all items on the bill.

Marketing

Market

WWW-TeleBel focuses on private consumers and small businesses with high telephone bills characterized by irregular usage (i.e., with upward peaks). Many of these clients spend a great deal of time on the Internet and use the latest communication technologies. In addition, there is another group of consumers who frequently use telephones to call family and friends abroad. The total market is estimated at 2 million customers. WWW-TeleBel should certainly be able to capture 40% of this market.

The service is supplied via the Internet and is therefore available worldwide.

Customers will be approached by means of a brochure enclosed with their printed statements. Attention will be drawn to the new service in standard radio and television advertisements as well. WWW-TeleBel will also be advertised on TeleBel's existing websites. Customers will be attracted by a one-off discount on their bill when they use the service for the first time.

Customers

WWW-TeleBel's projected customers consist of the aforementioned private individuals and small businesses with whom TeleBel wants to build a relationship based on mutual trust. This ensures that these clients will have good reason to stay with TeleBel. The target is to have approximately 800,000 customers using WWW-TeleBel.

Product/Service

The value that WWW-TeleBel adds is that customers can view their telephone bills any time they wish. In addition, their data will be available electronically, enabling them to use this information for other operations.

It is crucial that the quality of service of WWW-TeleBel is high. Information must be 100% correct and up to date at all times. The WWW-TeleBel webpage must be available at all times and must load fast and be intuitively easy to use—from registering online to accessing an account.

In addition, customers must be able to contact Customer Service easily when they view their statements online. For this purpose, there should be a "call-me-now" button. An e-mail option to contact Customer Service should also be available, and Customer Service should answer e-mail messages within 24 hours.

WWW-TeleBel is provided free of charge. Benefits to the company come from customer retention. As more new services are added over time, profits can also be made with an increase in turnover.

Environment

WWW-TeleBel can be developed and managed in-house.

Basic Conditions

Legal Aspects

In regard to customer data "learned" from online usage, WWW-TeleBel only registers the number of times the customer visits WWW-TeleBel and their behavior during those visits. In terms of privacy, this kind of information has a relatively low confidentiality level. The safeguards that need to be built in are therefore not drastic.

A policy must be developed with regard to the method of dealing with complaints about billed amounts. General terms and conditions for the use of the service must be drawn up.

Security Aspects

It is absolutely vital that WWW-TeleBel customers can only view their own user data and that their data cannot be viewed by any others. Security is therefore a very important issue. This can be achieved by using state-of-the-art security technology. Customer access will be protected by a password that customers choose during the online registration process.

Implementation

Human Resources

WWW-TeleBel is expected to increase the number of inquiries handled by Customer Service. These inquiries will be made by telephone and e-mail. Questions concerning billing and the like will not be a challenge for Customer Service. However, there will be new questions about the WWW-TeleBel application itself. Employees at Customer Service must be prepared for this, which means that all of them need to take part in a one-day introduction. However, for technical questions and problems beyond the scope of their training, Customer Service agents can transfer customers concerned to the WWW-TeleBel administrator.

The company expects that the increase of questions can initially be dealt with by employing one new employee. Another employee will be hired to answer e-mail queries. The latter will be assisted by a temporary worker during the initial phase.

To make full use of WWW-TeleBel, and to guarantee its perpetual high quality, a WWW-TeleBel product manager shall be appointed. This means that the new product manager must be recruited. The required effort for WWW-TeleBel is expected to be too great to allow it to be added to the tasks of a current product manager.

The management of WWW-TeleBel requires both functional and technical administration. Functional management can be dealt with by the employees already present. Nevertheless, an extra member of staff must be recruited for technical management.

Housing

WWW-TeleBel requires no extra housing. The additional employees can be accommodated in the existing building, but extra workspaces need to be created.

Resources

WWW-TeleBel can to a large extent make use of the Internet technology infrastructure that is already in place.

However, new software will need to be developed. This concerns modules for gathering the customer's billing data and showing them their latest TeleBel statement. These modules will be developed in the standard developing environments (i.e., C, Oracle, or Java). New modules will be linked to the existing billing systems via the message broker. There will be few changes to the existing systems because of the use of generic interfaces.

Processes

WWW-TeleBel requires major changes in the billing and service processes. Instead of bills being drawn up at set times, requests can now be made at any time. In other words, the trigger for drawing up bills must be changed.

For the service process, the introduction of WWW-TeleBel will imply an increase in the number of billing queries and their frequency will be less predictable and more spread out. The number of queries in the evening will also increase. In addition, there will be the new channel of e-mail.

Registration

WWW-TeleBel records data about customer visits to WWW-TeleBel. The data about customer visits is used to improve the service level and for marketing purposes.

Business Rules

WWW-TeleBel leads to the change that producing billing records no longer occurs at the fixed rate of every three months. It can also occur on demand.

Management

Responsibilities

The responsibility for WWW-TeleBel as a service lies with Product Management. The service is only available to existing customers. The responsibility for these customers does not change with the introduction of WWW-TeleBel. The adaptations in the processes for billing and service come under those who are responsible for these processes. The management of WWW-TeleBel is the responsibility of Operations.

Life-Cycle Management

WWW-TeleBel will have to be continuously renewed. The goal is to add a new "bell or whistle" every two months. These may include services such as advice about the most favorable type of subscription, an alert function when the account exceeds a user-defined level, customized statement form layout, and so on. This is one of the responsibilities of the WWW-TeleBel product manager.

Management Information

The following management information is desirable: (1) number of WWW-TeleBel users, (2) profile of WWW-TeleBel users, (3) shift in customer contact as a result of WWW-TeleBel, and (4) average number of visits to WWW-TeleBel per customer per month. This information can be derived from standard logging data.

Financial Analysis

Expenses

The calculation of cost for WWW-TeleBel is shown in Exhibits 5.6 and 5.7.

EXHIBIT 5.6	Investments in WWW-TeleBel (U.S.$ thousands)	
Investment Components	**2005**	**2006**
Software development	100	
Purchasing hardware	50	
Implementation	50	25
Marketing	50	25
Total investment	**250**	**50**

EXHIBIT 5.7	Annual costs of WWW-TeleBel (U.S.$ thousands)		
Annual Costs	**2005**	**2006**	**2007**
Operating costs	25	30	30
Human resources	100	100	100
Total annual costs	**125**	**130**	**150**

The net present value of investments and annual expenses amount to (assuming a 6% interest rate) $280,000 and $360,000, respectively.

Benefits

The benefits resulting from WWW-TeleBel are mainly in the area of customer relations. It is cheaper to hold on to a customer than it is to bring in a new one. In addition, WWW-TeleBel provides extra customer information. This may help increase turnover. Benefits have been summarized in Exhibit 5.8.

The net present value of the benefits amounts to $847,000.

EXHIBIT 5.8	Annual benefits of WWW-TeleBel (U.S.$ thousands)		
Annual Benefits	**2005**	**2006**	**2007**
Lower customer churn	200	240	240
Increased turnover	30	100	150
Total annual benefits	**230**	**340**	**390**

Financial Assessment

Exhibit 5.9 shows the results of comparing investments, annual costs, and benefits. It also shows that investment will be recovered in 2006, the break-even point year. Furthermore, another way to assess the investment is by calculating the NPV, as shown in Exhibit 5.10.

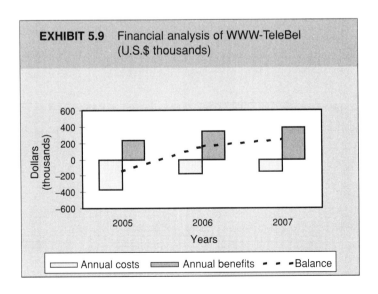

EXHIBIT 5.9   Financial analysis of WWW-TeleBel (U.S.$ thousands)

EXHIBIT 5.10	Net present value of WWW-TeleBel (U.S.$ thousands)
NPV Component	**2005**
Investment	−280
Annual costs	−360
Annual benefits	847
Total NPV	**207**

A third way to assess the investment is by using the Information Economics method. This method not only takes quantitative criteria such as return on investment into account, but also qualitative criteria such as the strategic need of the investment and the risks involved in not making the investment. In Exhibit 5.11, an IE assessment chart has been filled in for the business case of WWW-TeleBel.

EXHIBIT 5.11 IE Assessment Chart for WWW-TeleBel

Assess-ment factor	Operational Domain						Technology Domain					Plus (+) Score	Minus (−) Score	Total Score
	B1	B2	B3	B4	B5	B6	T1	T2	T3	T4				
	ROI	SM	CA	MI	CR	OR	SA	DU	TU	IR				
Weight factor	5	5	3	1	4	1	1	5	2	2				
Influence +/−	+	+	+	+	+	−	+	−	−	−				
Projects	Evaluation													
P1	4	5	4	2	5	3	5	3	5	1		84	30	54
P2														

TeleBel has put the limit levels for strategic need at 80 and for risks at 20. The exhibit shows that WWW-TeleBel has a strategic need (score 84); but WWW-TeleBel carries with it a relatively high risk (score 30), too. If the decision is taken to implement this project, it is important to take adequate measures to deal with the indicated risks. The risks in this project are mainly in the field of assessment factor T2 (Definitional Uncertainty), which means that demands and scope are not easy to clarify.

Planning

Starting Date

WWW-TeleBel can be operational on April 1, 2005.

Life Expectancy

The minimum expected life span of WWW-TeleBel is three years. In addition, WWW-TeleBel must be seen as a new means of communication with the customer, which can be expanded upon in a variety of ways. WWW-TeleBel, therefore, must be considered primarily as a growth model.

Note

1. IT Trends Institute and Verkenningsinstituut Nieuwe Technologie/ Sogeti, "Trends in IT: De Stand van 2001" (Sogeti, January 2001).

CHAPTER 6

Architectural Services

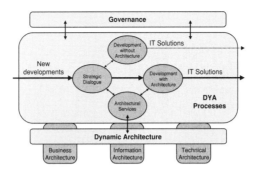

ARCHITECTURAL UPS AND DOWNS AT TELEBEL

Tom Alberts, the project leader at WWW-TeleBel, has been in a conference with his information engineer for the past two hours. WWW-TeleBel is under a small cloud and, if they are not careful, it could turn into a real thunderstorm. It started yesterday afternoon, when Tom's boss asked to see him. His boss said that management stressed again that WWW-TeleBel needed to comply with architectural requirements. If that was not the case, then management would have to take action. Considering that WWW-TeleBel was the IT department's showpiece, Tom's boss just wanted to hear from Tom that the project was not in trouble. Tom said what his boss wanted to hear, that the project met the architecture as much as was possible. Nevertheless, he had been warned and now he was asking his information engineer these burning questions: "How can we protect the project? Can we present our design in such a way that it complies with the architecture?"

Three floors up, Robert McCall, head of Architecture, is having a serious conversation with his top architect, Susan Forbes. Susan has just announced that she is leaving the company. This came as a shock to Robert, and he is now trying to understand why she made this decision, which is not difficult. Susan is very open:

> I want to do something that delivers clear results, to make a difference and provide real added value for my company. I really like designing enterprise architectures, and I feel it is very interesting work. The designing is not the problem. The problem is too little is done with it. Everyone says "good work" when we publish an architectural document. But then it's never used. Now and again, I feel I'm engaged in occupational therapy. And I'm not the only one that feels this way. I have discussed this with the others, and they feel the same way.

ARCHITECTURAL SERVICES:
DOING THINGS PROPERLY

Clearly, the architectural processes are not running smoothly at TeleBel. The policy on architecture states that it is important, and architectures are, indeed, drawn up. In practice, however, very little is done with it. The architectural way of thinking has not yet penetrated to the pores of the organization, and the architects are not properly connected to the IT development projects. What TeleBel needs is solid implementation of the Architectural Services process.

The goal of Architectural Services is to ensure that things actually get done properly. This does not end after drafting the architectural "instructions," but also includes the implementation of these instructions. A crucial aspect of Architectural Services is for it to be fully embedded in the organization's change process.

Architectural Services facilitates both Strategic Dialogue and Development with Architecture. The process is, therefore, a bridge between the business objectives and IT projects. The necessary architectural principles and models are supplied during the Strategic Dialogue process to work out the business cases. For this purpose, Architectural Services recognizes the two subprocesses of *managing architectural principles* and *drawing up models*, which are discussed in detail in the section titled "Architectural Services Supports the Strategic Dialogue" in this chapter.

Development with Architecture is supported with concrete outlines, guidelines, tools, and design choices that form the project-start architecture. For this purpose, Architectural Services recognizes the subprocess of *setting up a project-start architecture*, which will also be discussed in this chapter in the section titled "Architectural Services Supports the Development."

The subprocesses of Architectural Services are carried out by architects in close cooperation with the business case team and the project team. A characteristic aspect of the facilitating nature of these subprocesses is that the team of architects is usually involved in many different domain architectures. After all, each new business case requires a new piece of architecture, which must fit into the overall picture.

Maintaining an overview and making the relationships visible are of great importance. Before we continue to discuss the subprocesses of Architectural Services, we must first look at an important resource for the architect to maintain an overview: the architectural framework.

MAINTAINING AN OVERVIEW
WITH THE ARCHITECTURAL FRAMEWORK

In Chapter 3, we saw that architecture is a concept with many different aspects. For example, a distinction can be made on the basis of the object of architecture—namely, the things that the architecture relates to in the way of processes, data, applications, and the like. There is also a distinction between the various conceptual levels of architecture (from general principles to very specific models).

An architect has to deal with all these aspects in his or her work and must be capable of dealing with them properly. The architectural framework shown in Exhibit 6.1 is a useful tool. In this framework, the various objects of architecture have been set out on the horizontal axis. On the vertical axis, one can see the various conceptual levels of architecture. Each cell of the framework represents part of the enterprise architecture.

A word of warning is appropriate. We often have the tendency, as soon as we see a matrix, to want to fill in every cell. However, this is definitely not the idea in the architectural framework. Think of the just-enough, just-in-time principle and the goal-oriented approach of architecture. The framework is intended to provide domain architectures with a place in the overall picture and to make visible the relationship between the domain architectures. The framework is not meant to fill each cell from left to right and from top to bottom in a self-contained process in which it would become just another paper tiger. On the contrary, the framework provides the architect with the possibility of limiting him- or herself to specific parts when setting up an enterprise architecture, while preserving the overall picture. Which cells are relevant to the organization depends entirely on the situation and the objectives of the organization.

Refer again to Exhibit 6.1 and to the way the horizontal axis of the framework represents the different objects of the enterprise architecture. In Chapter 3, we saw that a common classification of enterprise architectures is the division into three sections: business architecture, information architecture, and technical architecture. These three sections are recognized by many architects. But another subdivision can be

EXHIBIT 6.1	Architectural Framework							
	Business objectives							
	Business architecture			Information architecture		Technical architecture		
	Prod/ service	Process	Orga- nization	Data	Appli- cation	Middle- ware	Plat- form	Net- work
1. General principles								
2. Policy lines								
3. Models								

made. A business architecture can consist of a product/service architecture, a process architecture, and/or an organizational architecture. An information architecture generally contains a data architecture and an application architecture. Finally, the technical architecture may include a middleware architecture, a platform architecture, and/or a network architecture. Each of these architectures has a different object of architecture such as products/services, processes, organization, data, and so on. For each of these objects, the framework has a different column. These columns are referred to as domain architectures.

Within a business architecture, information architecture, or technical architecture, we distinguish various domain architectures, each having a different object of architecture:

- *Product/Service Architecture*—The set of principles and models relating to the organization's product/service portfolio. These can be statements about the brands to be used, models for the creation of products by using standard components, standards with regard to life-cycle management of products and services, introduction policies with regard to new services, and the like.

- *Process Architecture*—The set of principles and models relating to the business processes of the organization that are necessary to achieve the business objectives. The process architecture indicates the main processes that the organization wants to distinguish; what requirements the processes should meet; what the interrelationship is between the processes; which processes should be outsourced; whether uniformity throughout the organization is desired, and the like.

- *Organizational Architecture*—The principles and models for the division of the organization's employees into departments and teams and for the coordination and control of activities. The organizational architecture may include the choice for a strong hierarchical organizational model or, instead, for a "flat" organization; for a division according to processes, expertise, or geography; central control or more of a network organization, and so on. Policies regarding collaboration with partners are also part of the organizational architecture.

- *Data Architecture*—The data architecture relates to the recording, management, and usage of the data that are relevant to the organization. The data architecture describes who is responsible for data and how it is arranged; who should have access to what data; whether data should also be accessible outside the organization; which data are shared and which are not; which standards are used for data exchange; and the like. The data architecture also contains, when appropriate, the definitions of companywide data and their interrelationships (i.e., company data model).

- *Application Architecture*—The principles and models relating to the organization's software applications. The application architecture provides the implementation principles of applications (e.g., components versus "best-of-breed" packages); the interrelationship between applications; the software environments to be used; which are shared applications and which are not; how authorizations are arranged, and the like.

- *Middleware Architecture*—Common organization-independent software components that allow applications and end-users to work together across the network such as message queuing, TP monitoring, ORB, RPC, EDI, XML. Middleware is the software that interfaces between the network and organization-specific applications. Part of the middleware architecture is the policy on middleware product resources, namely what middleware products the organization will use, when to use which product, and how these products work together.

- *Platform Architecture*—The platform architecture focuses on IT equipment. These include the mainframes, desktops, terminals, peripherals, and their operating systems. The platform architecture contains the resource policy for this equipment and sets standards with respect to scalability, availability (contingency plans), and compatibility.

- *Network Architecture*—The set of principles and models relating to connectivity of devices or the technical network of the organization (LAN, WAN). The network architecture contains prescriptive statements and models for the realization of the network (dedicated lines, private lines, telephone lines, wireless), network topology, bandwidth, communication and transmission protocols to be used, control and routing hardware and software, and so on.

At the top of the architectural framework in Exhibit 6.1, it reads "Business Objectives," indicating that all domain architectures serve one or more specific business objectives.

The horizontal axis of the framework indicates the various possible objects of architecture, which may lead to separate domain architectures. The vertical axis of the framework shows that each domain architecture can be divided into three conceptual levels:

1. The highest level is the level of general principles. These reflect the common vision of business and IT top management. The general principles apply to everyone and must, therefore, also be comprehensible to everyone.

2. The second level contains the concrete policy directives that give shape to the general principles. These directives are often more specialized than the general principles. They are a translation of the general principles into concrete details for each domain architecture. Standards and guidelines can be found at this level. Together, the general principles and policy directives are referred to as the *architectural principles*.

3. The third level is the level of the specific models. Depending on the object of architecture, they may take different forms. Graphic design often plays a major role here. The models are generally the realm of specialists.

In Chapter 3 we saw that, in addition to the dimensions of object of architecture and level of architecture, there is also a time aspect attached to architecture, the today, tomorrow, and next-minute architectures. Placing this time dimension on the architectural framework, we see that the general principles and policy directives are instances of next-minute architecture. They give definite direction to the decisions that must be made today. The models may serve as today architecture or as tomorrow architecture. These give a view of both the existing and the desired situation.

Recognizing the different levels of architecture provides a number of advantages:

- It facilitates communication at various levels within the organization:
  - The general principles are concise and can be used to communicate at every level of the organization. These principles provide clarity to the members of the business case teams.
  - The policy directives are eminently suited for communicating with members of the project teams. They constitute definite standards and guidelines that give direction to projects.
  - The models belong to the realm of specialists. They are used by a limited circle of specialists as a medium to transfer knowledge about a certain architecture (e.g., an application model).

- Accountability can be assigned in different ways:
  - The general principles rest with those who are responsible for policies: the top management.
  - The concrete policy directives are in the hands of those who are responsible for domains: business managers, information managers, or IT managers.
  - The models are entrusted to the specialists: the architects.

- For each architectural level, the level of coverage can be determined, such as the organization as a whole or a business unit (BU). The general principles apply to the entire organization, whereas concrete policy directives are drawn up for individual BUs.

- For each architectural level, what domain architectures to be maintained can be decided. In fact, one can even decide for each individual cell who will maintain it and with what frequency. (This subject is discussed when we deal with the subprocess of managing architectural principles.)

- The degree of detailing of a domain architecture may vary. Depending on the situation, it may be sufficient for some domain architectures if the highest level is only filled in, while other domain architectures require all three levels to be completed and elaborated. This depends entirely on the business cases that are being formulated.

Aspects such as security, quality control, management, and legal requirements are relevant for all levels of all domain architectures. Exhibit 6.2 uses TeleBel to illustrate how the architectural framework can be used.

EXHIBIT 6.2 Example of Architectural Framework		
General Principles	**Policy Directives**	**Models**
The customer has a single point of access for all his or her questions	Customer data is stored centrally (data)	Data model for customer data (data)
	Call center employees have achieved a high level of in-depth training (organization)	Profiles for call center employees (organization)
	Employees are supported by a customer-contact knowledge system (application)	Model of the customer-contact knowledge domain (application)
	Customer service process is supported by a workflow management system (application)	Workflow design (application)
We compete on quality	Process improvement is a continuous activity (process)	Process descriptions (process)
	Main criterion for hardware is reliability (platform)	Specifications (platform)
	Service is an important part of the services portfolio (service/product)	Services model (service/product)
	All employees will receive training in customer-orientation (organization)	Training plan (organization)

The domain architectures have interrelationships and influence each other: Choices made within the various domain architectures must match. However, we want to uncouple the domain architectures as much as possible to create freedom of movement. The architectural framework can be useful here:

- *All domain architectures are related separately to the business objectives.* As long as the business objectives are kept consistent (in the Strategic Dialogue), the domain architectures will not pursue mutually conflicting objectives.

- *The horizontal consistency is guarded for each conceptual level.* This means that a policy directive from the data architecture must not be in conflict with a policy directive from the application architecture. Each newly introduced policy directive must, therefore, be tested against the existing policy directives. The fact that all policy directives are derived from the same collection of business objectives should be enough to prevent most cases of inconsistency.

- *Domain architectures may set requirements for other domain architectures.* However, the way in which these requirements are dealt with in a domain architecture is screened off from the other domain architectures.

It is important to realize that the architectural framework does not, in itself, guarantee the coherence between the domain architectures. It is merely an aid toward maintaining an overview.

Having seen the usefulness of the architectural framework as an aid to the architect, we now look at the way in which the architect can use it to facilitate the Strategic Dialogue and the Development with Architecture.

ARCHITECTURAL SERVICES SUPPORTS
THE STRATEGIC DIALOGUE

Architectural Services supports the Strategic Dialogue by providing the necessary architecture for elaborating a business case. In particular, this concerns the relevant general principles and concrete policy directives for a rough outline of the solution and relevant models for performing the impact analyses. This has been translated into the two sub-processes of *managing architectural principles* and *drawing up models*.

Managing Architectural Principles

The process of *managing architectural principles* ensures that there is always a consistent set of architectural principles, which, in turn, serve as a guideline for elaborating business cases. This would include policy matters such as general statements, standards, guidelines, templates, and selection of resources. These architectural principles are the two highest levels of the architectural framework. We have translated the principle that architectural development should be business objective-oriented into the following procedure. When a business case is started, the team of architects collects the architectural principles that are relevant to the business case in question. Relevant architectural principles are those principles that provide direction when outlining the overall solution. If it appears that the current collection of architectural principles shows gaps, the team of architects will fill these. The new architectural principles do not merely apply to the business case at hand, but also to subsequent business cases. Although formulated on the basis of a specific business case, the principles apply immediately throughout the company and are used companywide until they are explicitly revoked. In this way, the enterprise architecture, as a whole, is given more and more shape. The team of architects, meanwhile, ensures that all principles remain internally consistent. It goes without saying that the team of architects will test any new architectural principles with those responsible for them (i.e., top management and those responsible for the domains).

No enterprise architecture will, therefore, be designed until there is a need for it in the form of one or more business objectives. However, the results of the design process will generally have a much greater reach than the business objective concerned. This applies clearly to architectures that have the nature of general facilities such as network and middleware architectures. The general principles and policy directives that arise from these (the first two levels of the architectural framework) are also set up for the organization as a whole. So we do not advocate throwing the generic character of enterprise architecture overboard. The architect always has a duty to look ahead to the future and not just deal with the here and now—he or she should take other developments within the organization into account. What is emphasized here is that the link with the organization's objectives is always made when developing and managing enterprise architectures.

The infrastructural character of a network architecture begs the question whether the design of such enterprise architectures should always be business objective-driven. Is it not a basic facility that simply needs to be provided irrespective of any specific business objectives? The answer is no. Even though, in present times, each modern enterprise needs a network, it is still advisable to deal with the design of this network within the framework of the business objectives. Only then can it be guaranteed that no facilities are provided that the organization does not need. First, the potential need of communication is determined, then the network is designed. If there is no business objective for which communication is necessary, then no network needs to be designed. If we forget about the principle of architectural processes being driven by business objectives, we soon run the risk of the infrastructure being out of line with its usage.

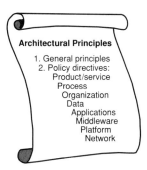

The subprocess of managing architectural principles results in a new version of the general principles and policy directives of the organization, as shown in the "Architectural Principles" list.

Drawing Up Models

The second subprocess within the process of Architectural Services, *drawing up models*, ensures that the business case team has the models at its disposal that are necessary for the execution of impact analyses. This concerns today architectures as well as tomorrow architectures (i.e., the third level of the architectural framework).

What triggers this subprocess is a business case that needs to be elaborated. Only models that are relevant for the business case are drawn up—and, where possible, use is made of models that are already present. As a rule, however, models are not maintained specifically for this purpose. This is a great difference with the general principles and policy directives. The reason for this is that the maintenance of models is particularly labor-intensive and that the amount of reuse of existing models appears to be disappointing. This applies, in particular, to models of the existing situation. It frequently occurs that, when a team tries to re-use a model, some of the details of the model are no longer correct. As the model is felt to be unreliable, the business case team decides to create the whole model anew. Besides, jointly drawing up a model has the additional advantage that it creates support and involvement.

Only in areas that are expected to be subject to a great deal of change are existing models maintained. Even then, this occurs when maintaining the models seems more efficient and effective than making new models at a later stage. The activities that are carried out in this process are focused on providing the necessary input for the business case, no more and no less.

It should be clear that the preference here is for drawing up required models rather than continuously maintaining existing ones. Therefore, it is important for the team of architects to have the ability to create models quickly whenever such modeling is necessary. To do so, they can use tools, such as TIPD (see Chapter 5 and Appendix A). Using templates, reference models, or checklists also accelerate the creation of models.

Models are not always limited to a single kind of object. To provide insight into the relationships between the various types of objects, overall models can be constructed. Exhibits A and B, which emerged from two different organizations, show a business architecture and a technical architecture respectively that combine different objects.

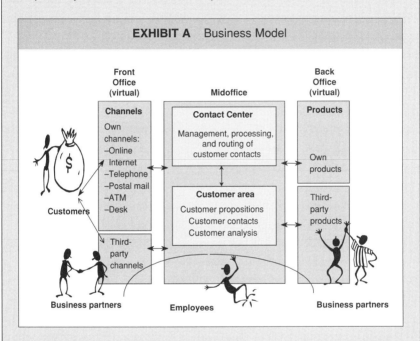

EXHIBIT A Business Model

Exhibit A demonstrates a combination of product/service, organization, and application. Exhibit B combines platform, middleware, and applications.

These examples also illustrate that the architectural framework of an organization should be determined situationally. On the basis of what an organization regards as important, it is possible to adapt this framework to the organization. The important thing is that there is clarity within the organization concerning the meaning of the various columns.

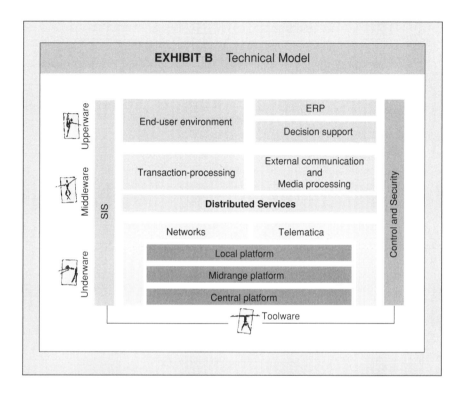

The final result of the subprocess of drawing up models is one or more models, as shown in the "Models for WWW-TeleBel" list.

To illustrate the application of the DYA approach to architecture, the example below describes the merger between two fictional insurance companies, CFA (Certainty for All) of New York and E-polis of Boston.

CFA specializes in offering property-and-casualty and life insurance policies through a network of brokers. CFA has a reputation as a respectable organization with solid products. If you take out insurance with CFA, it may be a little more expensive; but you never get a bad deal. The organizational structure and its IT systems are very product-oriented. There is a Property & Casualty business unit, which works with a large system that contains all policies and handles the settlement of insurance claims. This system also stores the data on the customers who have taken out Property & Casualty insurance policies. The system is written in COBOL and runs on an IBM mainframe computer under IMS. There is also a Life business unit, which, as the name suggests, deals in life insurance policies. For the administration of these policies, use is made of a standard software package on an AS/400 system. This package has been adapted over the years to the specific needs of CFA. The system contains data on customers who have taken out a life insurance policy. CFA has its affairs neat and tidy, but has trouble keeping up with developments in its field. CFA is losing market share.

E-polis is a so-called *direct writer*, selling insurance policies directly to customers without the intervention of any intermediaries. E-polis is a young organization whose aggressive style has won the company a considerable part of market shares. Private customers can take out insurance policies via the Internet and by telephone. E-polis sells many travel insurance and car insurance policies because of the attractive premiums. E-polis has a matrix organization with business units that focus on sales through a specific channel. There is an E-sales business unit, for example, that concentrates on selling via the Internet and a Telemarketing business unit that deals with selling over the telephone. In addition, there are business units that are responsible for product development and administration in the field of property-and-casualty and life insurance, respectively. E-polis has a large diversity of systems. The E-sales business unit, for example, uses Sun Solaris servers and NT servers for its website, a content management package, a security package, a personalization package, and an application for the registration of users. Use is made of MQ Series to collect customer data and policies from the databases of the Property & Casualty department and the Life Insurance department. The latter two departments have an application for the administration of property insurance policies and life insurance policies, respectively. The former application was developed in house with the aid of Oracle and runs on an RS/6000. The online life insurance application was developed in Microfocus Cobol workbench on an HP-UX. The Telemarketing business unit has a call center application under NT, which can also exchange data with Property & Casualty and Life systems via MQ Series.

The management of both companies have decided to merge on the basis of equality. The new company will merge the solid knowledge of the world of CFA with the power of E-polis, under a new name: Q&S (Quick & Secure). The new group expects to achieve tremendous cost savings by reorganizing overlapping activities and systems. Both companies have their own identity in the market. In addition, they use different channels to promote and sell their products. How can DYA help in such a situation?

The management of the new combination has two options:

1. Calling in an external consultants' agency to investigate existing procedures and existing systems and then to submit a proposal for new processes and the systems needed to support these. The proposal should make it clear which systems must be upgraded and which need to be parted with. The external agency should also draw up a plan that outlines how the desired situation can be achieved.

2. Implementing the DYA concept and choosing gradual upgrading and reorganization of processes and systems. Within the DYA concept, the first step is to have a number of sessions to identify common business objectives and to draw up business cases. General principles and policy lines are drawn up for the first business cases to be elaborated, which will also be determining factors for subsequent business cases and projects.

The management has chosen to implement the DYA concept. This provides for a gradual transition and ensures the greatest possible involvement from the two organizations, both from the business and the IT side. In addition, the former E-polis management has had a bad experience with outsiders drawing up a comprehensive plan: "The world is changing so quickly that, by the time the plan is finished, the world already looks different." Moreover, management fears that, with such a "Big Bang" transition, there will hardly be any space left for the development and launch of new products.

The first step, within the chosen approach, is to identify a number of business objectives. One of these business objectives is that a 30% cost reduction must be achieved within a period of three years. Another objective is that the market share of Life products must be increased from 4 to 6% within two years.

The first business case concerns increasing the market share by introducing three new life insurance products. Q&S feels that there is opportunity in the market as a result of the new tax system. Rapid action is essential. Q&S has chosen to introduce new products quickly and, at the same time, think about a structural solution. The new products will be introduced in a project using an offensive scenario, but an anticipatory scenario is launched simultaneously. Within the latter scenario, a new architecture is set up, with related processes and systems, for the life insurance products.

The chosen general principles include:

- Complete separation of product administration from customer administration and distribution channels.

- Both products and applications must consist of components that can be separately introduced.

The following policy directives are chosen:

- Platforms are standardized on Unix or NT.

- Oracle is used as a database management system for product administration.

- MQ Series is selected as middleware for the connections between product administration, customer administration, and distribution channels.

The knowledge gained in the offensive scenario proves to be useful in the anticipatory scenario. In the end, the decision is taken to introduce a new standard package for the administration of life insurance products. It appears to cater for both the products offered by CFA and by E-polis. The package uses an Oracle database, runs on an HP-UX, and consists of various components that can be implemented independently. MQ Series can be used to link the systems used by intermediaries to their own channels (the Internet and the telephone). The life insurance systems from the former CFA and E-polis are reorganized. E-polis's system can be separated relatively easily. In the case of CFA, more care was required because the life insurance system provided more functionality, including customer administration. This has been maintained for the time being.

The general principles and policy directives that were developed during this project are also applied to other business cases and projects. In this way, DYA provides a gradual growth path. By degrees, an enterprise architecture emerges that can be adapted constantly depending on the business objectives to be achieved.

ARCHITECTURAL SERVICES SUPPORTS THE DEVELOPMENT

In addition to the Strategic Dialogue, Architectural Services also facilitates Development with Architecture. This is done by means of the subprocess of *drawing up a project-start architecture*. This process provides the development project with concrete guidelines that can actually be used in the project and ensure that the results of the project fit into the larger picture.

The project-start architecture translates the general principles and policy directives into specific project guidelines. This way, the general enterprise architecture is tailored to provide solutions to the specific problems of the project. This means that the project-start architecture provides a very concrete and goal-oriented framework, within which the project must be implemented.

A project-start architecture is drawn up at the beginning of a project. This project-start architecture is then used to give the project a flying start because it provides basic conditions for the success of the project, such as the standards, models, and guidelines that it will use. These aspects no longer need to be decided during the project, but are handed over to the project with an explanation from the architects. In addition, the project team can gain a great deal of time because there is no need to coordinate extensively with other project teams: The links with products from other projects have been dealt with in the project-start architecture.

Project-Start Architecture

1. Environment model
2. Scope of the IT solution
3. Design choices
4. Standards and guidelines

It is preferable for the project-start architecture to be drawn up jointly by the architects and the project team together. By collaboration, they guarantee that the project team actually understands and endorses the architectural principles and their consequences. This makes it easier for the project team to keep to the guidelines. The architectural team benefits from the fact that the practical application of the architectural principles is tested properly.

The components of the project-start architecture are shown in the "Project-Start Architecture" list. A good way to arrive at the project-start architecture is to run through the choices that need to be made in the project that have an impact beyond the project and then make the appropriate decisions and include them in the project-start architecture.

The project-start architecture contains:

- An environment model that maps the field of interest, which includes the IT solution to be developed. This indicates the business context in which the IT solution is supposed to function.

- The demarcation of the IT solution, in both logical and technical terms, including any interfaces with other systems.

- The design choices that transcend the project. Only those design choices that have an impact outside the project are outlined in the project-start architecture.

- Standards and guidelines that apply to the project.

A good project-start architecture functions as a service-level agreement (SLA), both toward the organization itself and toward an external party, if the project is contracted out. The project-start architecture can be used to test whether or not the project delivers what was agreed upon.

The project-start architecture remains valid as a framework, even after the IT solutions have been taken over by the organization. This guarantees that any subsequent adjustments are also tested against the enterprise architecture.

At the end of this chapter, we have included the project-start architecture for WWW-TeleBel as an illustration. (More about project-start architectures is discussed in Chapter 7.)

ARCHITECTURAL TEAM

The process of Architectural Services is the architectural team's field of operation within the organization. Architects also collaborate within the business case team and review projects to make sure they are coordinated with the project-start architecture. Exhibit 6.3 shows that the architectural team is, therefore, like a spider in a web, holding all the threads.

The architectural team plays a key role, which is a reason to take a closer look at the composition of an architectural team. An important

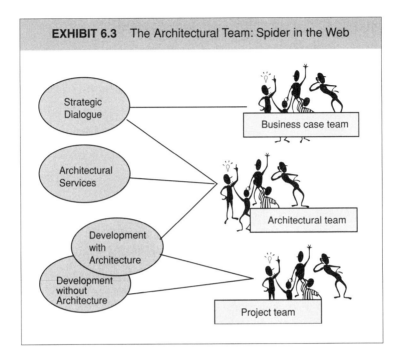

EXHIBIT 6.3 The Architectural Team: Spider in the Web

consequence of setting up an enterprise architecture, in a business objective-driven way, is that the Architectural Services process shows varying dynamics through the course of time. In times of great turbulence, there is a greater need for the services of architects than when the organization is sailing through smooth waters.

This means that there is not always an equal amount of work for the architectural team. Therefore, the appointment of a small, permanent core team of architects is recommended, which can temporarily be expanded during busy periods with employees from the standing organization. When the busy period comes to an end, the temporary employees can return to their regular duties. This has the additional advantage of a natural dissemination of knowledge, both about architectural principles and about operational issues. This is illustrated in Exhibit 6.4.

The dynamic character of the architectural team can be implemented as follows:

- There is a small core team of permanent architects. This core team will remain intact, even when there is very little to be done in the field of enterprise architecture. The core team is not much larger than one or two architects for each relevant domain architecture. The exact size, obviously, depends on the size of the organization.

- Specialists within the organization can be attached to the architectural team for a year, after which they will return to their previous place of work or, if they want and the possibility exists, they can move on to another job. Specialists who want to do something else, but do not know exactly what, may use such a year to determine how to continue.

- The void left behind in the standing organization must, of course, be filled. This can be done in various ways. As attachment to the architectural team never lasts longer than a year,

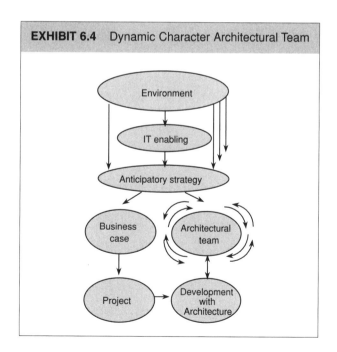

EXHIBIT 6.4 Dynamic Character Architectural Team

there is a regular supply of staff. These individuals may fill the voids. In addition, staff can also be hired temporarily. The fact remains that the organization must have some buffer to deal with this dynamic way of working. Organizations that work on the basis of projects, and occasionally lend their employees out to work on projects, are already accustomed to this approach. Allowing employees to work with the architectural team on a part-time basis can also be considered.

- To be able to put the temporary architects to work quickly, standards and templates are used.

It is clear that a great deal is demanded from architects. An architect, as we see him or her, must have many competencies. First, he or she must have subject-specific knowledge. It is impossible for an architect to have in-depth knowledge of all domain architectures. It is, therefore, useful to differentiate between specializations and to make at least a distinction between business architects, information architects, and technical architects. If desirable, one can even differentiate by domain architecture—and distinguish process architects, product/service architects, and organizational architects. The number of architects and the degree of specialization also depend on the size of the organization.

All architects should have an equal knowledge of the general principles. The policy directives need not be known by every architect. These demands are written in an understandable language, and they are quickly and easily accessible. The architectures at the third level in the architectural framework—the models—are created when necessary for a business case or a project. What matters most here is that an architect has the right skills to create the right models with the right scope. In addition to the specialization that has already been discussed, the following areas of competence are important for architects:

- *Architecture.* This is about the knowledge and skills necessary to be able to develop domain architectures. These include conceptual thinking, such as reasoning along multidimensional axes, modeling skills, and the ability to think in parallel (short-, medium-, and long-term) scenarios. The architect should also have a vision on the subarea in which he or she is working. Finally, an architect should be able to develop new concepts— or be able to "adopt" existing ones—and, subsequently, safeguard them.

- *Process Development.* This concerns the knowledge and understanding of changing business processes.

- *System Development.* This relates to the knowledge and understanding of carrying out system development projects, and the methods, techniques, and tools used to do so.

- *Technical Infrastructure.* This includes in particular the knowledge and understanding of hardware, networks and middleware, and the possibilities that modern IT offers.

- *Business Administration.* Business administration knowledge is equally important, including topics such as organization theory, business economics, and risk management.

- *Social Skills.* Social skills are of great importance for an architect. In a business case team, he or she has to be able to analyze the consequences of the business objectives to be achieved. He or she must be especially good at listening. In a project, he or she must be able to disseminate the selected principles and standards. He or she must be particularly good at convincing. In general, advisory and communicative skills are important here. The architect must be able to communicate with the business manager, the programmer, and the user.

- *Management Skills.* Finally, an architect must have management skills—that is, supervisory abilities as well as knowledge and experience in the field of stakeholder management and change management.

It is impossible for architects to excel in all the aforementioned competencies. For this reason it is important to create an architectural team that covers all competencies to a more than sufficient degree. After all, enterprise architecture is teamwork.

The architects obviously must have a place in the organization. It is important here that the architectural team operates as independently as possible. The architectural team should be positioned separately from the existing business and IT departments. The architectural team has the important task of creating a bridge between them. If the architectural team were placed in one of these two, the risk of having the interests of business or IT getting the upper hand would be great. (See Chapter 8.)

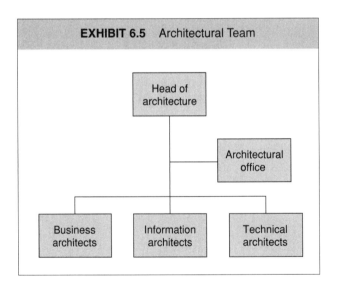

EXHIBIT 6.5 Architectural Team

The composition of the architectural team itself is shown in Exhibit 6.5, and the tasks relating to the various roles are summarized in Exhibit 6.6.

EXHIBIT 6.6 Tasks of the Architectural Team	
Section	**Tasks**
Head of architecture	Management of the architectural team
	Allocating architects to business cases and projects
Business architects	Setting up business architectures
	Following business and trade developments and translating those into possibilities for one's own organization
	Setting up project-start architectures
	Carrying out the role of supervisor (reviewing projects against the project-start architecture)
Information architects	Setting up information architectures
	In consultation with business and technical architects, making a translation from business to IT developments and vice versa
	Setting up project-start architectures
	Carrying out the role of supervisor (reviewing projects against the project-start architecture)
Technical architects	Setting up technical architectures
	Following IT developments and translating those into possibilities for one's organization
	Setting up project-start architectures
	Carrying out the role of supervisor (reviewing projects against the project-start architecture)
Architectural office	Managing architectures
	Managing current business cases and projects and the architects linked to them
	Managing the standards, methodologies, templates, and tools used by the architectural team
	Managing the architecture intranet site

ARCHITECTURAL SERVICES: COHERENCE AND AGILITY

Architectural Services forms a bridge between business objectives and the realization of IT solutions. By facilitating both Strategic Dialogue and Development with Architecture, direction is given to the way that business objectives are achieved; and IT solutions are guaranteed to fit into the organization as a whole. An Architectural Services process set up properly promotes coherence and agility.

Coherence is achieved by using the architectural framework to maintain an overview and clarify interrelationships. Coherence is further promoted by the project-start architecture. This ensures that the results achieved by a project fit into the larger unit as a whole.

Agility is achieved by not insisting on a companywide architecture on all fronts. Instead, enterprise architectures should be set up selectively—and they should be managed selectively, too. This will yield the first useful architectural products soon after the initial architectural efforts have been made. Consistent use of standards and templates accelerates processes. This applies not only to setting up enterprise architectures and launching projects, but also to processing products from others.

INTERMEZZO: WWW-TELEBEL'S PROJECT-START ARCHITECTURE

Environment Model

The environment model outlines the field of interest in which the IT solution must be developed. It is the business context in which the IT solution is expected to operate. The aim is to position the IT solution in a broader context. The environment model consists of a context diagram and relevant business processes.

Context Diagram

The Sales, Invoicing, and Customer Services departments are directly affected by the WWW-TeleBel project. Adjustments in the processes of these departments are within the scope of the project. To enable the service to work, further agreements must be made with the operator who provides the usage data. The customer, as a consumer of the service, is another important party.

The context diagram in Exhibit 6.7 shows the parties involved in the field of interest (inside the framework), and the external parties involved (outside the framework).

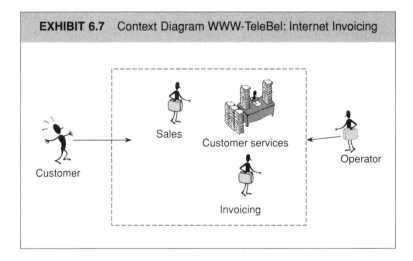

EXHIBIT 6.7   Context Diagram WWW-TeleBel: Internet Invoicing

Business Processes

The business processes involved, including human and other resources, are presented in this section. In the exhibits, the symbols represent process steps and the arrows represent triggers, information flows, or physical flows.

The following business processes are affected by WWW-TeleBel:

- Retrieving billing data over the Internet.
- Inquiring about billing data over the Internet.

The setup of these processes is illustrated in Exhibits 6.8, 6.9, and 6.10.

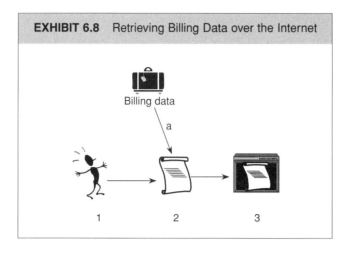

EXHIBIT 6.8   Retrieving Billing Data over the Internet

The main changes in the processes compared to the present situation are:

- The billing process provides billing data upon demand instead of at set times.
- Questions concerning billing data arrive at different times and also via e-mail.
- In the existing service process, new questions will come in concerning the WWW-TeleBel service.

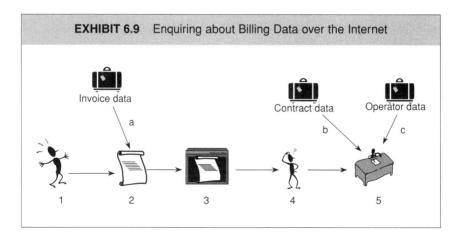

EXHIBIT 6.9   Enquiring about Billing Data over the Internet

EXHIBIT 6.10 Process Steps	
Retrieval Process	**Enquiry Process**
1. Consumer calls up billing data	1. Consumer calls up billing data
2. The bill is calculated	2. The bill is calculated
3. Billing data is shown	3. Billing data is shown
	4. Client asks a question concerning billing data
	5. Customer services answers the question
a. Outstanding bill items	a. Outstanding bill items
	b. Billing agreements with client
	c. Operator traffic data

Scope of the IT Solution

This section describes the scope of the IT solution that will be developed. Providing a clear scope prevents proliferation of functionalities, which would result in an unmanageable system.

Context Diagram for IT Solution

The context diagram for the IT solution in Exhibit 6.11 shows the IT solution in relation to its environment (other applications and users).

The IT solution to be delivered for WWW-TeleBel is developed according to the three-tier model. The IT solution will consist of two components:

- Drawing up the bill (composing bill).
- Showing the billing data on the Internet (TeleBel bill).

The *composing bill* component is a functional layer module, *TeleBel bill* is a presentation layer module.

There will be communication with the existing *calculating billing data* component. WWW-TeleBel users include both the consumers who use the service and the Customer Service Department that responds to consumer questions.

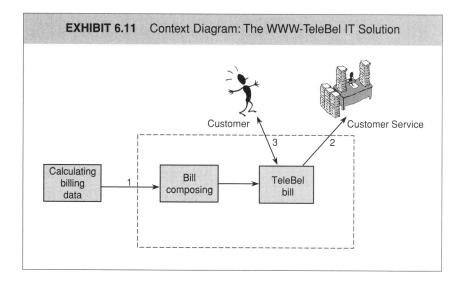

EXHIBIT 6.11 Context Diagram: The WWW-TeleBel IT Solution

Content of IT Solution

The functionality that the IT solution will offer is summarized in this section.

WWW-TeleBel contains the functionality indicated in Exhibit 6.12

Interfacing

The way the IT solution communicates with other parties—real people or applications—is shown in this section. Issues that are dealt with include the transmission protocol, communication protocol, message format, message content, volumes and frequencies, and availability.

EXHIBIT 6.12 WWW-TeleBel Functionality

Functionality	Realized in Component
Collecting current billing data	Composing bill
Drawing up overview	Composing bill
Showing billing data	TeleBel bill
Calling customer services	TeleBel bill
E-mailing customer services	TeleBel bill

The automated interfaces with the existing TeleBel components of WWW-TeleBel are shown in Exhibit 6.13. (The number refers to the numbers in Exhibit 6.11.)

This interface has the message format indicated in Exhibit 6.14.

EXHIBIT 6.13	WWW-TeleBel Application Interfaces		
Interface	**Content**	**Transmission Protocol**	**Communication Protocol**
1	Outstanding bill items	TCP/IP	XML

Interface	**Volumes**	**Nature**	**Availability**
1	2,000 p/day	Real Time asynchronous	24/7/365

EXHIBIT 6.14	Message Format for Outstanding Bill Items	
Data Group	**Field**	**Format**
Customer	Customer number	AN10
	ZIP code	NNNNN-NNNN
	House number	AN5
{Product/service}	Description	AN15
	Amount in dollars	N5
	Date	DDMMYYYY
{CDR}	Date	DDMMYYYY
	Starting time	HHMMSS
	Duration	N14
	Source	N12
	Destination	N12
	Amount in dollars	N5
Bill	Number	N10
	Discount arrangement	AN20
	From	DDMMYYYY

Technical Architecture

This section outlines the technical environment of the IT solution.

Exhibit 6.15 shows a graphic representation of the technical architecture for WWW-TeleBel.

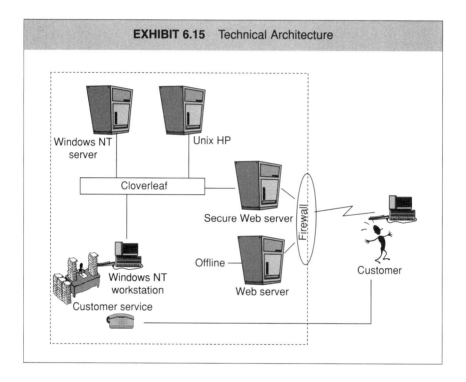

EXHIBIT 6.15   Technical Architecture

Design Choices

This section presents the design choices with regard to the IT solutions that transcend the project. Only those design choices that have an impact outside the project are mentioned here. This section also contains any specific agreements that have been made with the architectural team.

The following design choices that transcend the project have been made with regard to WWW-TeleBel:

- The TeleBel bill module must be expandable to include new services.
- For communication with existing applications, use is only made of existing *Application Programming Interfaces* (APIs).
- The existing Internet infrastructure (web server, firewall) will be used.

In addition, the following agreement has been made: If there are no suitable APIs for the required data exchange, then these will be realized by the supplying information system, in consultation with the architects.

Standards and Guidelines

This section provides the standards and guidelines used in the project.

Design and Development Standards

Exhibit 6.16 shows the design and development standards used for *calculating a bill.*

EXHIBIT 6.16 Design and Development Standards for Calculating a Bill	
Aspect	**Standard**
Design method	DSDM
Development method	DSDM
Programming language	Java
Message broker	Cloverleaf
Operating system	Unix
Hardware	HP

Templates and Guidelines

Within the WWW-TeleBel project, the following templates and guidelines will be used:

- Internet corporate style
- Business data model
- Interface description bill B03
- Guideline for the specification of APIs
- Guideline on security

CHAPTER 7

Development with(out) Architecture

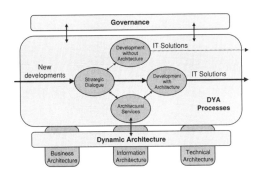

WWW-TELEBEL ONE YEAR LATER

"Oh no, not that too!" shouts Bill Henderson, the TeleBel product manager of Internet Billing, "That's the last straw. We should never have started WWW-TeleBel." Bill has just heard that Peter Simons, TeleBel's only Delphi programmer, is taking a sabbatical for a year. He wants to travel around the world. Peter was specially trained in Delphi to manage WWW-TeleBel. Without him, there is no one who can program in Delphi at TeleBel—and WWW-TeleBel was the first and, so far only, project to use Delphi. Now the company will have to find someone else. "Why was WWW-TeleBel not just developed in Java?" Bill asks himself. The company has several Java experts.

Peter's departure is not the only thing that bothers Bill about WWW-TeleBel. The system has been linked to the billing system in such a complex way that no one dares touch it anymore. As a result, Bill's two requests for changes in functionality have been ignored: The reason given is that it is too complicated and too risky for the existing application. Wasn't anyone looking ahead and thinking about the future when they designed WWW-TeleBel? Bill wonders. And not to mention the cost! The break-even point should have been reached after one year. Well, that didn't happen.

Bill doubts whether this point will ever be reached. Maintenance is too expensive because everything must be done by specialists. Almost all of the tools used for WWW-TeleBel are used nowhere else within TeleBel. No, WWW-TeleBel worked perfectly for the first three months but now—a year later—it is becoming a permanent source of trouble.

DEVELOPMENT WITH(OUT) ARCHITECTURE: DOING THE RIGHT THINGS THE RIGHT WAY

When the objective to be achieved is clear, the required IT solution is developed. In general, this must be done faster than fast. The client will not wait and just as easily move to another supplier. But what is often forgotten is that the story does not end when the system has been delivered. On the contrary, that is the real beginning. An application that has been developed in six months can remain in use for five to ten years. In those five to ten years, it must be kept running and be adapted to changes in the business. In addition, the application is generally not used in isolation. Data that is stored in the application will, at some time, also be needed elsewhere in the company. The application must fit in with the other parts of the company. All of these issues are easily forgotten when, forced by the market, the only guideline is faster than fast. The result is that the IT solution may be up and running in no time, but problems start to arise after about six months, and these get bigger. This is what happened at TeleBel. Maintenance became expensive because the company did not use its standard development environment. Moreover, there is a great continuity risk—revealed here when the only Delphi expert decides to take a year off. Adaptability is restricted because this was not taken into account when the interfaces were designed.

In the creation of IT solutions, the process of *Development with(out) Architecture* takes into account the total life cycle of the application to be supplied—not merely the first, relatively short development phase. By considering this life cycle, the result is an IT solution that is maintainable, that fits in with a company's environment, both today and in the future, and can grow with the company. In short, such solutions are a joy rather than a burden, not only now, but in the future, too.

As we will see, however, it is possible to think of situations in which an organization chooses, by way of exception, not to develop with architecture. This chapter, therefore, not only discusses development with architecture, but also development without architecture.

In the process of Development with(out) Architecture, doing the right things—Strategic Dialogue—and doing things right—Architectural Services—come together in doing the right things right.

THREE DEVELOPMENT STRATEGIES

Development with Architecture strives toward an IT solution that integrates with the other parts of the organization. The application that is delivered must not only work well immediately after delivery, but during its entire life cycle. This means that we do not just develop for today, but also for the future. In this way, we create information systems that are prepared for the future and have a high anticipatory capacity. Adjustments can be made quickly, allowing for quick responses to changes in the environment.

There are those situations in which a rapid response is required, in which there is no time to think about the future and only the present matters. The focus has to be on a single specific aim or on one part of the organization at the expense of ignoring the rest of the organization for the moment. Time, in such situations, can become such a dominant factor—and architecture is easily forgotten.

This type of situation is inevitable in this day and age, when the predictability horizon gets shorter and an organization increasingly faces surprises. Whether an organization is capable of providing timely answers to such surprises depends on two variables[1]: (1) the speed at which the opportunity or threat emerges and dies down again, and (2) the time that the organization needs to plan and implement its response. Even though a dynamic architecture reduces the time to respond adequately, situations do exist in which the response time is too short to consider the architectural aspect; this may even happen with an architecture that has been created with agility because it is impossible to be prepared for every eventuality. Occasionally, organizations experience situations in which projects are forced to run without architecture because of the time available. There are ways to deal with this. Even in organizations that make architecture compulsory, projects may choose not to comply and find workarounds to not using architecture. Sometimes this is done openly, the architecture simply being ignored. Sometimes it is done in a more concealed way, with the project paying lip service to the architecture, but otherwise just trying to go its own way. Whatever happens, it is completely beyond the reach of the architect and with all the consequences this brings.

For this reason, the DYA concept acknowledges the process of consciously deviating from the architecture—development without architecture—alongside development within the architectural framework—development with architecture—only for special cases. By including deviation from the architecture in the control process as a whole, architecture is no longer ignored. It is done only when there is a good reason, and the process is controlled. Working without architecture is embedded in the organization. This makes it possible to subject working without architecture to (its own) rules and restricting any negative effects.

Within the process of Development with(out) Architecture, there are three development strategies:

1. Anticipative
2. Defensive
3. Offensive

The *anticipative strategy* is the default strategy. In this strategy, projects comply with the architecture with the aid of a project-start architecture. By applying this strategy, the organization arms itself structurally for the future. In addition to the anticipative strategy, there are the *defensive strategy* and *offensive strategy* as shown in Exhibit 7.1.

In the first situation (on the left in the exhibit), the organization finds itself in a defensive position that requires a short-term solution. The organization has its back against the wall because its very existence is at stake. The environmental condition, which requires the organization to react, is so threatening that an appropriate response must be made at all costs. This results in an ad hoc IT solution with high problem-solving content, but which is not directed at the future or any other business objectives. What this IT solution does do, however, is achieve the urgent business objective on time, at all costs. This is the defensive strategy.

In the second situation, the organization finds itself in an anticipative strategy. In this case, the organization chooses a structural solution, resulting in an IT solution with a high anticipatory capacity: It takes into account that there will undoubtedly be new demands and require-

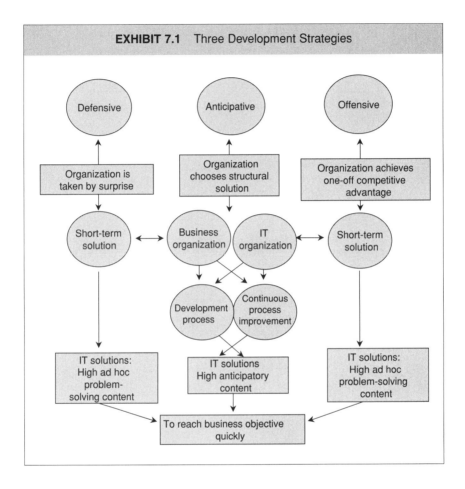

EXHIBIT 7.1 Three Development Strategies

ments in the future. The IT solution is also prepared for the fact that other parties may want to link up.

In the offensive strategy, the third situation, the organization sees an opportunity for achieving a one-off competitive advantage to which the principle of "now or never" applies. If the organization fails to act now, then the opportunity will have gone. Again, speed is essential to get there before the competition does. The organization itself takes the initiative. This is another example of ad hoc problem-solving.

The difference between the defensive/offensive strategy and the anticipative strategy is that the defensive/offensive strategy creates a high ad hoc problem-solving content, whereas the anticipative strategy creates a high anticipatory content. The difference between these two is illustrated by the following statements:

"If you want to keep a man from starving, give him a fish" (high ad hoc problem-solving content).

"If you want a man to be independent, give him a fishing rod and teach him how to fish" (high anticipatory content).

ANTICIPATIVE STRATEGY

The goal of an anticipative strategy is to achieve a structural IT solution with a high anticipatory content. A characteristic aspect of the anticipative strategy is that it looks beyond the single business objective for which the project was initiated. The tool to achieve this is the architecture. Exhibit 7.2 illustrates the anticipative strategy.

In the anticipative strategy, there is close cooperation between the continuous process of Architectural Services and project-based Development with Architecture. As described in the previous chapter, Architectural Services provides the project-start architecture that forms the framework for Development with Architecture. In Development with Architecture, the desired IT solution is realized. This always occurs on the basis of a business case that has been set up within the Strategic Dialogue. The projects are carried out according to the standards and guidelines of the project-start architecture.

The project team commits itself to that project-start architecture. During the development phase, progress made by the project team is frequently tested against the project-start architecture. This means that architectural aspects are part of the progress reports. The project-start architecture constitutes the framework within which the project team works. This framework is focused completely on the project and ad-

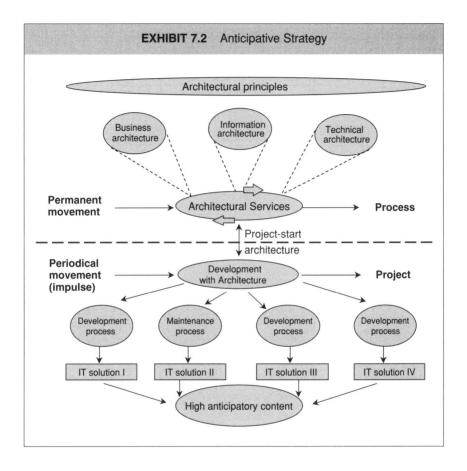

EXHIBIT 7.2 Anticipative Strategy

dresses all relevant issues that transcend the project. These can include the standards, guidelines, and templates that are used as well as certain design choices that are relevant outside the project. The extensiveness of the project-start architecture depends entirely on the situation and the degree in which organization-wide architectural principles have been formulated. Those issues, which the organization believes should be dealt with in a particular way, are included in the project-start architecture—no more and no less. The basic content of the project-start architecture is presented in the list below.

The project-start architecture ensures that the final result delivered by the project fits into the information systems as a whole. Also, because management and flexibility requirements are considered, the project-start architecture ensures that the entire life cycle of the application is taken into account during the development of the IT solution.

The project-start architecture, if properly applied, also has a positive effect on the speed of development. The project team can concentrate all its energy on creating the solution. Using a project-start architecture has the following advantages:

- Time-consuming discussions about the tools to be used and the required techniques are unnecessary. As time passes, the experience in using standard tools and techniques will increase. The project team can focus its attention on the objective instead of on the means. This facilitates a rapid start of the project.

- Additionally, many choices have already been made in the project-start architecture, making it clear right from the start which competencies are needed. This makes it possible to find the right people for the project.

- Another aspect of the project-start architecture that can mean a considerable acceleration is that the project team does not lose a disproportionate amount of time holding coordinating sessions with other projects and parties. This has already been dealt with in the enterprise architecture.

- Finally, time is saved by the project team having all impact analyses and accompanying models of the business case team. Part of the definition study and functional design, products of traditional development methods, has already been done. For example, the scope and direction of the solution are already known. There is also a so-called context diagram and an overall process model.

Introducing new IT solutions need not always mean developing tailor-made solutions. Increasingly, the choice is made to implement an off-the-shelf package. This occurs, in particular, with applications for which efficiency is more important than the ability to be distinctive.

The question that now arises is whether there is such a thing as implementation of packages under architecture that is analogous to development under architecture? The answer is yes. We can look at the implementation of packages under architecture from different angles—and there is the issue of fitting a package into the architecture. First, it is possible to draw up the standards and guidelines for the selection, purchase, and handling of packages, such as the following:

- The selection process is carried out by the business case team.

- Packages are evaluated on points that have been described on the checklist for package selection. This includes the ability to exchange data with other information systems, the capacity of the package (both with regard to the number of simultaneous users and the number of transactions), the data model used in the package, and such issues as support during implementation, user guides, and training.

- Packages are not adapted.

- Packages are only purchased when they have been successfully implemented in at least five other known organizations in the same field and at least one of these organizations is comparable in size to our organization.

- Packages are only purchased when they are, to a certain degree, viewed as being standard in our field.

When it has been decided to purchase a package, the next question is how it should be fitted into the enterprise architecture as a whole. Linking the package to other information systems plays a major role. Rarely will a package be used by itself. It is more likely that it will need data that is supplied by other applications and that it, in turn, supplies data to other applications. This exchange of data must be unequivocally specified. It may be necessary to place a translation module between the two systems if the sender and receiver do not speak the same language. Many packages contain internal databases that must be used. For this reason, it is important to safeguard against duplication of data, with the additional risk of duplicating maintenance efforts and data inconsistencies. It must also be decided whether the internal database of the package is to receive the status of a source file or secondary database. If the package is labeled a *source file,* then this will place extra-high demands on the data model of the package. As is the case with one's own development work, these types of issues can be dealt with by using a project-start architecture.

Obviously, the positive effects of the project-start architecture can only be realized if the architecture is actually used. To achieve this, a number of measures can be taken:

- If possible, the project-start architecture should be created jointly by architect and project leader. This guarantees that there is a workable project-start architecture for the project team, which is also supported by the project team. Responsibility for the architecture remains with the architects.

- The project-start architecture is included as an integral part of the project definition. The project leader is not merely accountable for completing the IT solution within the budget and time allotted, but also for keeping to the architecture.

Throughout the development phase, the project results are regularly tested against the project-start architecture. A useful tool for this is the so-called *building permit* shown below. The building permit is given at the start of the project by the lead architect. Development work cannot start until the building permit has been issued.

Having drawn up the design, the building permit must be renewed before work may continue. After implementation, it will be decided whether the project was carried out in accordance with the building permit and whether supplementary actions are necessary.

Building Permit	
Project name:	*WWW-TeleBel*
Project code:	*TB0012*
Client:	*J. Hernandez, Product Development Director*
Project manager:	*T.R. Alberts*

Building Permit *(Continued)*

Documentation inspected

Project definition WWW-TeleBel version 1.0
Project-start architecture WWW Telebel version 1.2
Decision document Business case

Is there an approved project-start architecture?	(yes) / no
Is there an approved business case?	(yes) / no
Is there an approved project proposal?	(yes) / no

Remarks:

All required documents are available and approved by the
management of Private Customer Market.

Advice

Issue building permit?	(yes) / no
Architect:	S.M. Forbes
Date of advice:	January 2, 2005

Motivation:

All requirements have been met.

Project will start with creating a standard infrastructure for Internet services.
It is, therefore, an important project from an architectural point of view.

Building Permit *(Continued)*

Decision

Building permit has been	(issued) / refused
Lead architect:	R.J. McCall
Date of decision:	January 3, 2005
Motivation / conditions: *See advice.*	

The full building permit, including the extension after the design phase and after implementation, appears at the end of this chapter.

The project-start architecture as an important guideline cannot be overstated. There are, however, situations in which it is necessary to deviate from this guideline—and that should happen in consultation with the business case team and, in particular, with the architects. At the same time, parties involved will look at any possible consequences of this deviation for the rest of the information supply. If necessary, domain architectures will be adapted. The project-start architecture will also be adapted to the new situation to make sure that it describes the current situation. This is important, too, because the project-start architecture will be handed over to the maintenance team upon completion.

Working with project-start architectures has the additional advantage of being easier to outsource parts of the development work while the organization still remains in control. This is because the project-start architecture provides clear frameworks. As long as the developing party adheres to that framework, the organization can be sure that the

IT solution that is ultimately delivered meets the objectives and fits the information systems as a whole.

For similar reasons, it is also easier to hire occasional specialists. The project-start architecture guarantees mutual cohesion between the specializations. A comparison can be made with the construction business, where the carpenter, the bricklayer, and the plumber each have their own specialist work—ultimately, however, they build one house.

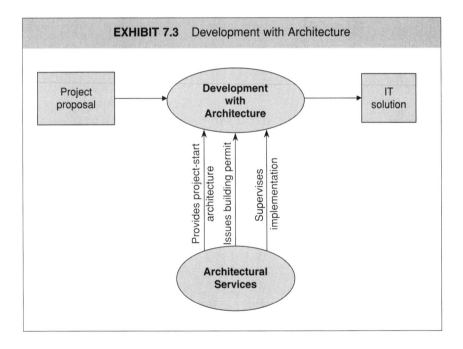

EXHIBIT 7.3   Development with Architecture

The interaction between the Development with Architecture process and the Architectural Services process is shown in Exhibit 7.3. It can be summarized in the services that Architectural Services provides to the Development with Architecture process:

- It delivers a project-start architecture.
- It issues a building permit.
- It exercises supervision on the implementation of the project.

OFFENSIVE STRATEGY AND DEFENSIVE STRATEGY

The offensive strategy—or defensive strategy—is followed when time is a dominant factor, making it impossible to take every architectural aspect into account. These two strategies have a great deal in common. The difference between them is that the defensive strategy is used when the organization has its back against the wall and is forced to defend itself. The offensive strategy is used when the organization has discovered an opportunity and wants to seize it aggressively. The offensive strategy is, therefore, carried out from a position of attack.

Nowadays, we can see an increasing need for offensive strategies. Because of greater transparency and the disappearance of historic barriers to joining the market, competitive advantages are more temporary. A temporary competitive advantage is attractive for a client, but can be contested and copied by the competition relatively quickly. Agility, for this reason, is essential. Hence, the need may arise for a short-term solution that will result in an ad hoc IT solution with a high problem-solving content.

The defensive strategy approach does not differ from that of the offensive strategy. The difference is in emphasis. Because the organization takes the initiative in the case of the offensive strategy, there is generally more freedom of choice.

The defensive/offensive strategy is characterized by time being the all-decisive factor in the development process. Anything can be changed, including the working method, and even functionality or quality, but not the final date of the project.

The first step in this strategy is to determine when the IT solution can be ready, and when the date is set and nobody can touch it. The schedule, then, can be adhered to by means of a "time-boxing" mechanism.

A *time box* is a time span in which the start date and the end date are fixed. That means, the work must be completed within that particular time span. Time-boxing is not activity-oriented, but product-oriented—the aim simply is to reach an objective by the deadline set. How this is done is entirely up to those who do the actual work. The activities are not important, however, the result is.

No matter how good one is at planning, there are always unforeseen circumstances or setbacks within a project that jeopardize the schedule. But time-boxing does not allow any extensions. The date is "sacred." For this reason, we need some compensation. This compensation is usually functionality. We add quality for the defensive/offensive strategy. This is illustrated in Exhibit A, which shows the four control variables that are connected to the development route: time, money, functionality, and quality.

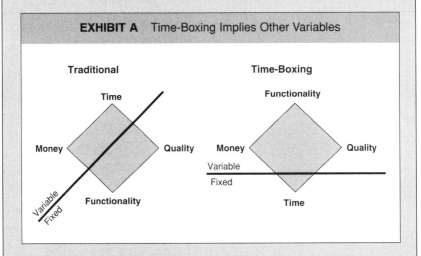

EXHIBIT A   Time-Boxing Implies Other Variables

The left side of the exhibit shows that in traditional system development, functionality and quality are fixed. There is a decision document that describes exactly what must be delivered. This is what the project promises to do. If the project runs into trouble with regard to the schedule during implementation, this means that more time and money will be needed. Obviously, this does not mean time and money are unlimited. The business case must remain positive: If it becomes apparent during the project that the expected results cannot be achieved, the project should be reconsidered.

On the right side of the exhibit, we see that, in the case of time-boxing, only the time is fixed. If the project schedule runs into problems, the solution must be sought in money, functionality, and quality. For this reason, functional requirements and quality requirements are prioritized. Requirements with the lowest priority are the first to be given up.

The defensive/offensive strategy requires the possibility to decrease functionality and quality when it becomes clear, during the course of the project, that the final date may not be reached. The MoSCoW-principle can be used for this.[2] MoSCoW is an acronym for setting priorities with regard to the requirements of a system. The capital letters stand for:

Must haves—those requirements that are essential for the system. If these requirements are lacking, the system is unusable and worthless. The *Must haves* provide what is referred to as the "minimum usable subset."

Should haves—important requirements that might also have been regarded as essential if there had been enough time available. If absolutely necessary, the system can do without them.

Could haves—those requirements that can be omitted more easily in a partial delivery of the system.

Want to haves, but will not have this time round—those requirements that can wait until the next round.

Although in the defensive/offensive strategy the work deviates from the architecture, this does not mean that control is unimportant. On the contrary, it is precisely because control is important that the possibility of working outside the architecture is explicitly embedded. However, the control is different from that in the anticipative strategy. What the project-start architecture and building permit are for the anticipative strategy, the *management letter* is for the defensive/ offensive strategy.

The management letter is drafted at the start of the defensive/ offensive strategy. It is written by the project manager, with the assistance of an architect, and signed by the client, the lead architect, and the project manager. The management letter clearly states the way money, functionality, or quality should be sacrificed to meet the deadline.

Because the defensive/offensive strategy does not work with a project-start architecture, the project result will not fit as well into the information system (or systems) as a whole. In addition, very little attention is paid to the issue of maintenance. Chances are great that the solution will show cracks and can even cause obstructions in the organization. It is, therefore, important to limit the life expectancy of the result supplied and to simultaneously start the development of a structural solution according to the anticipative strategy. This is also included in the management letter.

Management letter
1. Declaration
2. Project data
3. Scope of the project
4. Agreements on implementation defensive/offensive
5. Agreements operation
6. Agreements start anticipative strategy

A warning is necessary here. If parties fail to state and start an anticipative strategy at the beginning of the defensive/offensive strategy, chances are that it will never happen. After all, with the defensive/ offensive strategy in place and producing the desired results, the organization has the functionality that it needs—so, it might be asked, why waste funds and human resources to recreate the same functionality? That the delivered product will not function over time and inevitably cause major problems is not always regarded as sufficient reason by the business management. It will wait and see. Therefore, it is important to start the anticipative strategy in concert with the defensive/offensive strategy. The project assignment should have it explicitly stated that the project managers are not just responsible for realizing the temporary IT solution, but also for removing it again at a predetermined date. By allowing the project manager to also manage the anticipative project, risks are better controlled. This has the added advantage of using the knowledge accumulated during the defensive/offensive strategy in designing the anticipative strategy.

To work successfully with the development strategies, it is essential for each project that it be absolutely clear whether it is an anticipative, defensive, or offensive strategy. Only then can the accompanying procedure and control method be used effectively. The question is, of course, when it is decided how to classify a project. In principle, this can be done at various moments, but it is always somewhere between the moment when management orders the creation of a business case and the moment when management approves the accompanying project proposal. The default procedure is to start from the anticipative strategy. If the business case team, elaborating the business case, arrives at the conclusion that time is so short that the team should change to a defensive or offensive strategy, this will be put before management, who then need to make a decision. If the decision is taken to switch to the defensive or offensive strategy, the business case team will discontinue its activities—and the project team will start its work. The project team may, naturally, consist of some of the same individuals. The first thing the project team will do is draft a management letter and have it signed.

An example of a management letter, applied to WWW-TeleBel, has been included at the end of this chapter.

PROJECT TEAM

Working under architecture places extra demands on developers and, in particular, on designers. Different demands are put on the anticipative strategy and the defensive/offensive strategy.

Anticipative Strategy

In the anticipative strategy, designers have to conform to the standards, guidelines, methods, and tools that are prescribed by the project-start architecture.

A project will receive not only a project-start architecture, but also a business case, including all the models that have been created for it. This means that part of the work that was left to the designer has already been done. One of the consequences of this is that subject-specific knowledge becomes more important for the designer. He or she must be able to interpret the models quickly and translate them into a design.

A third consequence of working with architecture is that it demands a certain basic attitude. Where the designer could concentrate fully on achieving as efficiently as possible the specific business objective for which the project was started, he or she must realize now that there are matters that also count alongside the business objective. The designer will have to include elements in his or her design that are important to other (future) projects (e.g., generic interfaces and reusable components).

Finally, the designer will have to work with the organization's architects. Not only when he or she works with the project-start architecture, but also during completion of the project, when the designer hands over to the architectural team the models that he or she has adapted.

Defensive/Offensive Strategy

The defensive/offensive strategy sets its own demands on the project team. The team has more authority in decision making than in the anticipative strategy. To achieve the necessary agility, the objective and scope of the system are defined at a relatively high conceptual level. During the development phase, the project team makes a decision on the exact content. The team would only delay matters if it had to contact higher management for every decision. The team and, in particular, the team leader, must be able to deal with this responsibility.

In addition, the emphasis is clearly on the frequent supply of products: The team is fully concentrated on supplying products within a predetermined time. They are not told how to create those products. The team must decide for themselves. This requires a certain amount of creativity. Also, there is a need to be decisive when it comes to breaking off the creative process at the right time to actually produce the solution. This requires a high level of stress resistance.

As was the case in the Strategic Dialogue, multidisciplinary cooperation is essential in the defensive/offensive strategy. The various disciplines are "thrown into a pen" to come up with a solution within the time set. Social skills are, therefore, very important. There must be a willingness and ability to understand and respect each other's disciplines.

MAINTENANCE WITH(OUT) ARCHITECTURE

Working under architecture does not stop at the initial development phase. Maintenance of the IT solutions, at least in the anticipative strategy, is carried out under architecture as well. There are two ways in which maintenance is related to architecture. On the one hand, maintenance is bound by the framework of architecture. On the other, maintenance sets its own demands on architecture that is directed at a manageable IT environment.

Theo Thiadens distinguishes between infrastructure and the applications that use the infrastructure as objects of maintenance.[3] The infrastructure itself is divided into technical infrastructure and informational infrastructure. The technical infrastructure supports all tasks in the field of storage, processing, transport, and the import and export of images, speech, and data. The objects of maintenance include servers, networks, and workstations with their operating systems and network software. Objects of maintenance, in the informational infrastructure, include development and maintenance tools.

Within the maintenance of applications, a distinction is often made between functional maintenance, application maintenance, and technical maintenance. Functional maintenance concerns the functionality that is to be supplied with the aid of IT. Application maintenance is about realizing the requirements of functional maintenance in the applications. Technical maintenance keeps the application running.

Enterprise architecture plays a role in all of these maintenance aspects. When the maintenance team takes on an application, the transfer includes not only the usual system documentation, but also relevant parts of the project-start architecture that relate to the application being taken on for maintenance (within a project, several applications can be developed or adapted). These parts of the project-start architecture also serve as a framework for maintenance purposes. For example, functional adaptations in an application will only be honored if they remain within the limits of the application as indicated by the architecture. Major maintenance work that does not fit within the project-start architecture must be coordinated with the architectural team.

An important advantage for application maintenance is that the system documentation that is provided will be more standardized and, therefore, is more recognizable and quicker to process by the maintenance team.

The maintenance team is not merely the recipient of architecture. Maintenance also places demands on development. This may vary from demands in documentation to demands in the way that applications are set up. Application maintenance, for example, may demand that applications be developed using clearly defined independent components that make adaptations easier to implement in the future. Functional maintenance indicates which functionality should be achieved in which application. Technical maintenance places demands that promote sustained performance and availability of applications. Maintenance may also formulate requirements for the way in which interfaces between applications are created. After all, proliferation of interfaces is one of the main causes of maintenance problems and the maintenance effort in general. In consultation with the architectural team, such requirements may be included in the domain architectures of the organization (level two of the architectural framework, the policy directives). Via this route, they end up in the project-start architectures of the individual development projects.

Enterprise architecture also plays a major role in infrastructure maintenance in establishing resource and supplier policies for the components of both the technical infrastructure and the informational infrastructure (hardware, networks, development, and maintenance tools). The architectural team draws up these policies together with the maintenance team.

Different rules apply to the offensive strategy and the defensive strategy, which, in many cases, lead to temporary solutions being realized. This also places limits on the maintenance to be carried out. In this way, maintenance limits itself to keeping the application running for the duration of the period stated in the management letter. Functional adaptations will not be carried out.

DEVELOPMENT WITH(OUT) ARCHITECTURE: COHERENCE AND AGILITY

In the Development with(out) Architecture process, IT solutions are created that are needed to achieve the business objective that has been determined in the Strategic Dialogue. The process is supported by the Architectural Services process. The standard situation is that development is carried out with architecture. For this purpose, the project team receives a project-start architecture. Occasionally, the decision is taken to develop without architecture. This process is also embedded in the organization in the form of an explicit strategy. The management letter ensures that any negative effects of working around architecture are kept within limits. If the Development with(out) Architecture process is structured well, it will contribute to both coherence and agility.

Coherence is achieved in the anticipative strategy by keeping to the project-start architecture. In the defensive/offensive strategy, striving for coherence is more or less abandoned. The negative effects of this, however, are limited by restricting the life cycle of the solution and by starting a simultaneous anticipative strategy. This eventually promotes coherence after all, even if it does not happen immediately because of time constraints.

Agility is achieved in the anticipative strategy because many issues, which can cause the project team to lose time, have already been catered to in the project-start architecture. The team gains time by not having to occupy itself with discussions on methodology, by not having to coordinate everything with everybody in the organization, and by not having to discover, halfway through the project, that they overlooked a host of dependencies. If, in exceptional cases, the anticipative strategy is not fast enough, there is still the possibility of resorting to a defensive or offensive strategy to come up with a rapid solution.

INTERMEZZO I:
A BUILDING PERMIT FOR WWW-TELEBEL

The building permit is issued to a project by the lead architect. Issuing a building permit means that the project complies with the architectural requirements to a sufficient degree. The building permit is issued at the beginning of a project and subsequently extended when crucial milestones have been reached (or revoked if the project no longer meets the requirements). The building permit is issued or extended after the following phases:

1. Drawing up the project proposal
2. Drawing up the design
3. Implementation

Project Data

Project name:	WWW-TeleBel
Project code:	TB0012
Client:	J. Hernandez, Product Development Director
Project manager:	T.R. Alberts

Phase: Drawing Up Project Proposal

Documentation Inspected
Project definition WWW-TeleBel version 1.0. *Project-start architecture WWW-TeleBel version 1.2.* *Decision document Business case.*

Is there an approved project-start architecture?	(yes) / no
Is there an approved business case?	(yes) / no
Is there an approved project proposal?	(yes) / no
Remarks: *All required documents are available and approved by the* *management of Private Customer Market.*	

Advice	
Issue building permit?	(yes) / no
Architect:	S.M. Forbes
Date of advice:	January 2, 2005
Motivation: *All requirements have been met.* *Project will start with creating a standard infrastructure for Internet services.* *It is an important project from an architectural point of view.*	

Phase: Drawing Up Project Proposal *(Continued)*

Decision	
Building permit has been	(issued) / refused
Lead architect:	R.J. McCall
Date of decision:	January 3, 2005
Motivation / conditions: *See advice.*	

Phase: Drawing Up the Design

Documentation inspected
Functional design WWW-TeleBel version 2.1. *Project-start architecture WWW-TeleBel version 1.2.*

Conformity with Project-Start Architecture
Design conforms with project-start architecture.

Critical Points of Attention
Security aspect is still insufficiently worked out.

Agreements Made
Security aspect to be elaborated upon February 10, 2005.

Advice

Extend building permit?	(yes) / no
Architect:	S.M. Forbes
Date of advice:	February 3, 2005

Motivation:

Design conforms completely with project-start architecture. I have faith in the security aspects being ready on time. Clear agreements have been made concerning this.

Decision

Building permit has been	(Extended) / Refused
Lead architect:	R.J. McCall
Date of decision:	February 4, 2005

Motivation / conditions:

See advice.

Permit has been issued under the condition that the security aspect will be dealt with on February 10, 2005.

Phase: Implementation Completed

Documentation Investigated

Project-start architecture WWW-TeleBel version 1.3.
Technical Design WWW-TeleBel version 2.2.

Conformity with Project-Start Architecture

Realization is in accordance with the new version of the project-start architecture.

Phase: Implementation Completed *(Continued)*

Changes in Project-Start Architecture

The project-start architecture has been adapted. This was done in consultation with the architects. The adaptations include the realization in C++ instead of Java. Motivation for this was the availability of usable standard modules in C++.

Unfulfilled Agreements

All agreements have been fulfilled. The security aspect was dealt with on time.

Agreed-Upon Actions

No further action required.

Architect	S.M. Forbes
Date	April 1, 2005

INTERMEZZO II:
A MANAGEMENT LETTER FOR WWW-TELEBEL

Declaration

The signatories of this management letter, being the client, the project manager, and the lead architect for the project, as described in the project data, hereby agree that the aforementioned project will be carried out according to the conditions stated in this management letter.

The project manager is responsible for the implementation of the project. By signing this management letter, the client and the lead architect declare to be in agreement with the formulated conditions and to facilitate the completion of the project to the best of their abilities.

Project Data

Project name:	*WWW-TeleBel*
Project code:	*TB0012*
Client:	*J. Hernandez, Product Development Director*
Project manager:	*T.R. Alberts*
Lead architect	*R.J. McCall*

Scope of the Project

Date upon which project will be completed	February 15, 2005

Project objective

Implementation of the possibility for clients to view their bills via the Internet at any given moment.

Agreements on Project Implementation According to the Defensive/Offensive Strategy

If Necessary, the Following Measures Should Be Taken in This Order

1. Exceeding the budget up to 50%.
2. Not realizing the functional requirements in the appropriate order (could haves, should haves). Priority of the various functional requirements has been shown in Appendix A.
3. No documentation.
4. No use of the standard developing environment.
5. Not realizing the quality requirements in the appropriate order (could haves, should haves). Priority of the various quality requirements has been shown in Appendix B.

Agreements on Project Implementation
According to the Defensive/Offensive Strategy *(Continued)*

The Following Requirements Will Not Be Compromised

1. DSDM will be used as a design method with further specification because of the defensive/offensive strategy.
2. Use will be made of the existing Internet infrastructure unless this results in an unacceptable delay.

Agreements Regarding Operation

Operation of the Project Result

1. The information system to be supplied in this project has a lifespan not extending beyond May 1, 2006. The project manager is responsible for removing the system on this date.
2. The project result will not be extended with extra functionality.
3. Management of the project results will be limited to keeping the system running and maintaining availability.
4. The maximum number of users is 2,000. With more applicants, a stop will be introduced.

Agreements Regarding the
Start of the Anticipative Strategy

The Following Structural Measures Are Taken

1. As of March 1, 2005, an anticipative strategy will be started. The signatories will be the client, project manager, and lead architect for the anticipatory project.
2. For the benefit of the anticipative strategy, a business case will be elaborated from February 15, 2005 until March 1, 2005. The client will be responsible for this.

Signature for approval by the client
Date   Name   Signature

Signature for approval by the project manager
Date   Name   Signature

Signature for approval by the lead architect
Date   Name   Signature

Notes

1. H.I. Ansoff, "Managing Surprise and Discontinuity: Strategic Response to Weak Signals," *Zeitschrift für betriebswirtschaftliche Forschung* 28 (1976), pp. 129–152.
2. DSDM Consortium, *Dynamic Systems Development Method*, version 3 (Farnham, UK: Tesseract Publishing, 1997).
3. T. Thiadens, *Beheer van ICT-voorzieningen*, 3rd rev. ed. (The Hague: Academic Service, 1999).

CHAPTER 8

Governance

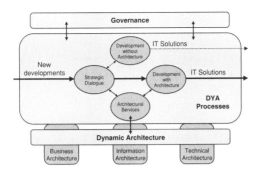

DEADLOCK FOR TELEBEL

"Tell me this isn't true." Richard Fairbanks, director of TeleBel, looks up in desperation, "This is unbelievable," he says, taking another look at the project overview that is before him on the table. It was difficult enough to get the overview. He had to wait five weeks to get a full picture of every project. And what he got in the end did not make him a happy man. The number of projects alone came as one kind of shock—122—which was far too many. Where was the focus? Although TeleBel had been working under architecture according to DYA for two years, Fairbanks now had doubts about whether projects were being carried out in accordance with the anticipative strategy—or with any strategy. The strategy followed was not specified in the overview that he just read. Richard has a feeling that there could be quite a few "irregular" projects in this batch. Two years ago, TeleBel started with their spirits high and a great deal of enthusiasm. There have been clear positive results. Projects are no longer started just like that. There is more cooperation between business and IT, and the number of development environments has decreased by 30%. But it seems as if some things have gone out the window again. Richard has the impression that projects are increasingly going their own way—under the pretext of offensive strategy. An anticipative strategy might get initiated, but, one way or another, it often gets bogged down. No, Richard thought, this is not the way to do things yet. Obviously, the organization still does not "get" the importance of working with architecture. It is time to crack down again. Richard reaches for the phone.

SUCCESSFUL PROCESSES DO NOT JUST HAPPEN

The TeleBel company is finding out the hard way that processes do not work well by themselves. The company implemented the three processes of Strategic Dialogue, Architectural Services, and Development with(out) Architecture. However, the initial bloom of enthusiasm has faded and the company has slipped back into its old habits. TeleBel has discovered that it is not enough to implement processes, that good control is indispensable as well. Responsibilities must be assigned unequivocally. The many different developments within the organization must be coordinated. There must also be a monitoring system to ensure that the desired results are achieved. Both processes and control require continuous attention—that is, *governance*.

Governance means control and command through organizational and procedural measures that coordinate the activities of the organization in such a way that they contribute fully toward achieving the business objective.

Various aspects play a role here:

- Responsibilities and authority should be assigned without ambiguity. If it is not clear who is responsible for what and who should make decisions, everybody will go his or her own way and the organization will end up in a kind of vacuum in which nothing happens and everybody waits for everybody else.

- Governance is maintaining an overview of and giving direction to all ongoing projects within the organization. In the TeleBel example, there are 122 projects. This may seem extreme, but there are organizations that easily reach this number. One way or another, some sort of overview must be maintained to ensure that developments do not overlap, neutralize, or impede each other. Maintaining an overview is also required to use scarce resources in the best possible way.

- To ensure that all guidelines and procedures that have been agreed upon are used, a monitoring system is necessary.

- After all architectural processes have been set up, it is important to keep monitoring whether the objectives set by the organization are being achieved. The cycle of observing, evaluating, and adjusting is a continuous process. If this aspect is neglected, there is a danger of the organization getting bogged down in processes and procedures that have no added value.

> It is useful to check from time to time whether existing processes still provide added value. Many organizations, for example, experience the phenomenon of the "unused report." In Department A, there is an employee whose task it is to draw up Report X on a weekly basis and to send it to Department B. In Department B, there is an employee who receives Report X from Department A every Monday morning. She puts this report in a filing cabinet with the other Report Xs—and not one person reads it and no one ever wonders whether it is even necessary to draw up Report X.

RESPONSIBILITIES AND AUTHORITIES

Assigning responsibilities and authorities is a crucial requirement for successfully working under architecture. This should start with the decision taken by the organization to work under architecture. Such a decision has far-reaching consequences for the way in which the entire organization works, and it can, therefore, only be made by top management. This decision must be taken explicitly, jointly by business and IT, and must then be disseminated convincingly throughout the organization. There is no such thing as "working under architecture on the sly."

> **The Balance between Control and Self-Organization**
>
> Governance is not a new phenomenon. For centuries, people have been working together in organizations, attempting to coordinate their activities. Willem Mastenbroek provides an interesting overview of the history of organizations.[1] He describes how they have shown a balance of tension between control and self-organization from the Middle Ages onward. In the beginning, mankind was not very good at self-organization and self-discipline and needed a great deal of explicit external and, in particular,

detailed direction. The person in charge not only dictated exactly what had to be done, but also when and how it had to be done. Over the centuries, however, self-organization increased, enabling control to take on a different form. Control became more implicit and less comprehensive. Today, much can be left to the internal direction of the employee. Control now takes the shape of providing frameworks in which employees have a certain freedom (freedom within restraint). As a result, control has not lessened over the centuries, but has become more focused. Control in a restricted, specific area is combined with greater independence of individuals and teams within limited frameworks.

This evolution toward a more distinctive role for both control and self-organization is still continuing. One of the driving forces behind this development is the great mutual dependence that is emerging in business today. We no longer do everything ourselves and, therefore, enter into partnerships with other parties. This makes us dependent on others. In addition to one's own autonomy, being able to work together and negotiate with other parties have become important skills. We clearly see this in e-business. To be successful in e-business requires being able to provide a unique added value—autonomy—in combination with being able to create effective collaboration—interdependency. The balance between autonomy and interdependency is the more abstract variant of the balance between self-organization and control. Being able to deal with this balance properly is of decisive importance for success in e-business.

This means that when we establish governance, we need to find the right balance between self-organization and control. This can be translated into the following principles:

- Top management gives the organization a clear and unambiguous focus, but does not dictate how work should be carried out—that is, directing on results rather than on procedures.

- The responsibility for procedures is assigned to the lowest possible level in the organization.

- Control is achieved by reaching agreements on results to be exchanged.

- Giving instructions is done sparingly. Instructions are only given if there are clearly demonstrable reasons for doing so in terms of business objectives.

> • Employees and teams are assessed on their added value in achieving the business objectives.

Once it has been decided to work under architecture, there are a number of issues for which responsibility must be assigned:

- Business objectives
- Content of the architecture
- Projects
- Architectural processes

Business Objectives

First, there is the responsibility of setting up the business objectives. Top management is responsible for setting business objectives for the organization as a whole. Middle management (a term used to indicate the management of the various units, such as BU or IT managers) is responsible for translating these overall business objectives into objectives for each individual unit.

Content of the Architecture

Second, there is responsibility for the content of the enterprise architecture. Top management is responsible for the content of the highest level of the architectural framework, which consists of general principles. At this level, all statements must be approved by top management. If there is a danger of inconsistencies emerging in the general principles, top management will have to make choices to restore consistency.

Once it has been decided to work under architecture, there are a number of issues for which responsibility must be assigned:

Middle management is responsible for the content of each individual domain at the second level of architecture, the policy directives. Obviously, these should be in line with the general principles provided by top management. Responsibility for domain architectures that transcend the units, such as data, is assigned by top management to one of the middle managers.

The architects, finally, are responsible for the third level of the architectural framework, the specialist models. The architects also work within the frameworks of the higher levels. It is important that their contribution to the organization be assessed on the degree to which projects comply with the enterprise architecture and the degree to which this compliance contributes to the business objectives—and not only on the architectural documents they produce. After all, this is not about producing paper tigers.

Even though management is responsible for the two highest levels of the architectural framework, they may allocate maintenance and monitoring to the architectural team. The content, however, remains a management responsibility.

Projects

The third area of responsibilities concerns the implementation of projects. Depending on the level, the decision to launch projects lies with top or middle management. The first formal decision about IT development is taken when management assigns the elaboration of a business case. Management makes this decision only when the proposed idea contributes to achieving a specific business objective. This is called the *first level of approval*. The next formal decision making occurs when the business case has been elaborated and has yielded a concrete project proposal. This is the *second level of approval*. If management orders the implementation of the project proposal, any further direction of content is carried out via the project-start architecture. The latter is created jointly by the architects and project manager, however the responsibility lies in the hands of the architect. The project-start architecture gives the project team frameworks within which it can move freely. Independent decisions are made as long as the project team adheres to the project-start architecture.

This procedure is followed in the anticipative strategy. This is the default strategy for every project. If time pressures force the organization to adopt a defensive or offensive strategy, doing so requires the explicit approval of management. Switching to a defensive or offensive strategy is possible up until the moment when the project proposal is approved by management. At that time, the project is definitely classified as falling into one of the three strategies. Approval for a defensive or offensive strategy can, therefore, only be requested somewhere between the first and second level of approval.

Architectural Processes

Finally, there is the responsibility for the architectural processes. This lies with top management, which is responsible for the implementation of the Strategic Dialogue, Architectural Services, and Development with(out) Architecture. In this capacity, top management ensures that work is being done according to the processes and that these still meet their objectives.

The four areas of responsibility are shown in Exhibit 8.1. Related to the assignment of responsibilities is the question of who answers to whom. This is usually arranged in the organizational structure. Of particular relevance is the structural organization of the architects. There are various possibilities. One option is to divide the architects among the business sections: The business architects are in the various business units, the information architects and technical architects in the various IT departments. The other extreme is to place all architects—both business and IT—together in a single department at a level immediately below top management. There are also a number of inter- mediate variants.

In choosing the best organizational structure for the architects, several aspects should be taken into account:

- Cooperation between business, information, and technical architects is essential. Any organizational barrier for such cooperation must be avoided.

- Architects must have a wide view that extends across the boundaries of individual projects and department interests. The architect is responsible for maintaining cohesion and the organization's interest as a whole. The organizational structure that forces an architect into conflicts between his or her department and the organization as a whole should be avoided.

- Architects must not end up in an "ivory tower" where they lose themselves in architectural efforts that nobody wants. In other words, architects must stay focused and closely involved with everything that is going on in the organization.

EXHIBIT 8.1 Responsibilities for the Architectural Processes

	Top Management (Business + IT)	Middle Management (Business + IT)	Architect (Business + IT)	Project Portfolio Management	Project Manager
Organization's business objective	Accountable		Advice and maintenance		
Unit's business objective		Accountable within the framework set by organization's objectives	Advice and maintenance		
General principles (level 1 architecture)	Decision		Advice and maintenance		
Policy directives (level 2 architecture)		Decision within the framework of level 1	Advice and maintenance		
Models (level 3 architecture)			Decision within the framework of levels 1 and 2 and maintenance		

Business case	Decision		Advice		Advice
Strategy	Decision		Advice		Advice
Project	Assigning project	Assigning project within the framework set by organization's objectives	Creating project-start architecture and supervising architecture		Decision within the framework of the assignment and architecture, and implementation
Project portfolio	Decision	Decision within the framework set by the organization's objectives		Monitoring and maintenance	
Strategic dialogue	Decision and implementation	Implementation	Advice, maintenance, and support during implementation		
Architectural services	Decision		Advice, maintenance, and implementation		
Development with(out) architecture	Decision		Advice, maintenance, and support during implementation		Implementation

The first two aspects listed above constitute arguments that support grouping all architects in a special department at a level immediately under top management. This would promote cooperation, and independence would be guaranteed. This, however, has an ivory tower risk. Measures must be taken to counter this effect. For example, if an organization chooses to have a small core team, as described in Chapter 6, that can be supplemented as needed with employees from other departments, these employees can prevent the architects from being isolated—or straying, too. Keeping strictly to the facilitating character of architectural development is another way of preventing architects from ending up in an undesirable position of isolation.

In addition to drawing up instructions and procedures, there are other ways to stimulate people into exhibiting desirable behaviors.

An important tool is compensation. Making undesirable behavior costly is one way of making desirable behavior attractive for those involved. This can be done in the following way. The anticipative strategy, which is the standard, makes use of the architectural infrastructure of the organization. The cost of this basic infrastructure is paid for by the business units according to a fixed rate, irrespective of whether the units use it. If they use the basic infrastructure to the full, they will easily recover the costs. If they choose not to make full use of the basic infrastructure, their costs will be doubled: the costs of deviation and the fixed rate for the basic infrastructure. If necessary, this effect can be reinforced by adding on an extra monthly charge for deviators for as long as their divergence continues. The extra costs will be removed only when top management feels that the unit concerned has rectified the deviation and is once again running with the pack. Whether this approach works in practice depends to a great extent on the culture of the organization.

Another way to stimulate desirable behavior is to streamline objectives. Many coordination problems arise from differences in objectives. A well-known example of this phenomenon is the architect whose objective is to have the entire set of information systems running optimally and the project manager who has the objective of realizing his or her project within the time and budget constraints set. In this setup, the project manager will always make compliance with the enterprise architecture subordinate to achieving a project result within the allocated time and budget. One way of dealing with that is to bring the objectives of the various parties closer together. For example, the project manager can be given explicit instruction by the client to comply with the architecture. Of course, this only works if one of the client's objectives is working under architecture, which eventually takes us back to top management.

Behavioral codes and values also constitute a powerful tool for control. As behavioral codes and values are embedded deeply in the organization, they are generally a strong guideline for all activities. If the code within the organization is to meet the requirements of architecture, based on the belief that it is good for the organization, then this is one of the best guarantees that development under architecture will actually take place. The difficulty with this type of control is that the behavioral codes and values present within an organization cannot be easily changed.

COORDINATION OF DEVELOPMENTS

An important element of control, both with respect to content and to resources and planning, is coordination of all current developments. In the case of content coordination, enterprise architecture plays an important part. After all, the primary aim of the enterprise architecture is to guarantee cohesion among all developments (i.e., architecture as a management tool). This is one of the responsibilities of architects. In collaboration with the project team, the architects draw up a project-start architecture for every project—a specific detailing of part of the architectural framework. Keeping the architectural framework consistent as a whole guarantees that the project-start architecture fits into the larger picture. That projects do not have conflicting goals is ensured by relating each project to business objectives established by management. If management draws up new rules, these will always be checked for consistency with existing objectives.

Compliance with the architecture allows for better risk management of development projects. Beginning with the use of the project-start architecture, the risk of the project result not fitting into the larger picture has been strongly reduced. After all, if the project adheres to the project-start architecture, the result is guaranteed to fit in with the information systems as a whole. Compliance thus ensures better coordination among all IT components.

The project-start architecture also reduces the chances of IT elements creeping in that should be classified in the category of "hobbyhorse," with hidden costs such as training, needing a special maintenance group, and delays caused by unfamiliarity.

Using business cases also reduces risks. As business and IT jointly draw up the business case, the chances of misunderstandings and differences of interpretation are much smaller. The various parties involved experience the process of creating a business case together and, therefore, know why certain choices have been made. In addition, the involvement of technical specialists ensures from the start that the requirements and wishes drawn up can actually be met.

The fact that projects are only started to achieve a clearly formulated business objective, which fits in with the other business objectives of the organization, and that decision making takes place on the basis of business-economic grounds, greatly reduces the chances of embarking on the wrong projects. This means that fewer projects will be discontinued prematurely because it is clear that they are not useful or there is no longer a budget.

Finally, the risk of IT solutions being impossible to maintain or only at high costs is also reduced. After all, maintenance is part of the project-start architecture. Using standards limits the number of development environments to be maintained and, for that reason, keeps them manageable and affordable.

With respect to the coordination of resources and planning, it is useful to set up project portfolio management. This means keeping an overview of all current activities taking place, including business cases and projects. As every project must be approved by management, both at the start of the business case and at the start of the project, these moments of decision are ideal times for *registering* the projects. Registering includes dealing with a number of key issues such as status, strategy, staffing, and planning. The implementation of these activities can be discussed by a project portfolio team that is specially created for the purpose. The project portfolio team supports management by providing information, but management remains responsible.

MONITORING

It is not recommended that agreements be made at the beginning of a process and then to lean back and wait until it has reached the end. If there is a long time between the beginning and the end, experience has taught to keep a finger on the pulse. Management and architects have various tools at their disposal for doing so.

For projects carried out as part of an anticipative strategy, the building permit can be used. Projects receive a building permit at the beginning, which needs to be extended after the design phase and must be ticked off after implementation. Building permits are issued by the architects. The project portfolio team is a safeguard ensuring that building permits are applied for and extended by projects at the right time.

In addition, enterprise architecture can be included as a permanent part of the regular progress reports.

One way to quickly provide an overview of the progress of an IT development project is the "Project Dashboard" shown below. For each aspect—finance, planning, architecture, and project result—several questions need to be answered. On the basis of the answers, the aspect concerned receives a green, yellow, or red light. A green light indicates that there are no problems. A red light points to major problems—and measures need to be taken. A yellow light indicates a danger zone. There are some problems that the project itself can hopefully solve. However, alertness is necessary.

Project Dashboard

1. Finance
1.1 Is the project staying within the budget? -- ☐ ☒ ☐ ☐ ☐ ++
1.2 Are there no unexpected setbacks? -- ☐ ☒ ☐ ☐ ☐ ++
1.3 Are setbacks expected? -- ☒ ☐ ☐ ☐ ☐ ++

2. Planning
2.1 Is the project still on schedule? -- ☐ ☐ ☒ ☐ ☐ ++
2.2 Is the project staff adequate? -- ☐ ☒ ☐ ☐ ☐ ++
2.3 Are the required subject matter
 experts available? -- ☐ ☐ ☐ ☒ ☐ ++
2.4 Are the required resources available? -- ☐ ☒ ☐ ☐ ☐ ++
2.5 Will the deadline be reached? -- ☐ ☐ ☒ ☐ ☐ ++

3. Architecture
3.1 Have the requirements of the project start
 architecture been met? -- ☐ ☐ ☐ ☒ ☐ ++
3.2 Have existing standards been used? -- ☐ ☐ ☐ ☒ ☐ ++
3.3 Have architectural adaptations
 been carried out? -- ☐ ☐ ☒ ☐ ☐ ++
3.4 Is there a building permit? -- ☐ ☐ ☐ ☐ ☒ ++

4. Project result
4.1 Is the project result in accordance
 with the agreements? -- ☐ ☐ ☐ ☐ ☒ ++
4.2 Is proper documentation available? -- ☐ ☐ ☐ ☒ ☐ ++
4.3 Has implementation been arranged? -- ☐ ☐ ☐ ☒ ☐ ++
4.4 Has maintenance been arranged? -- ☐ ☐ ☐ ☒ ☐ ++
4.5 Have the conditions been met? -- ☐ ☐ ☒ ☐ ☐ ++

The dashboard is completed periodically (e.g., once a month) by the project manager. Calculating the color of the lights is done according to a fixed algorithm, which may be fairly simple or quite advanced. For example, each question may be given a certain weight. This weight is multiplied by the answer, which varies from very bad (double minus = 1 point) to very good (double plus = 5 points). The total score determines which color of the light is appropriate (e.g., less than 8 is red; between 8 and 16 is yellow; above 16 is green).

For projects carried out as part of a defensive or offensive strategy, agreements are made on the quality, functionality, and life cycle of the project result. These are recorded in a management letter, which is signed by the client, the architect, and the project manager. The project portfolio team ensures that agreements made in the management letter are fulfilled.

PROCESSES ALSO REQUIRE MAINTENANCE

As is the case with applications, the story does not end with the implementation of the architectural processes. Once the Strategic Dialogue, Architectural Services, and Development with(out) Architecture have been implemented, they must be maintained. Are processes running as planned? Are objectives being achieved? Are processes efficient? These questions are valid not only after implementation, but also after some length of time. Process management is keeping processes running— and improving them if necessary. It is a continuous process.

Because process management is continuous, responsibilities should be assigned. An owner must be appointed for the processes, who will be responsible for the processes both in terms of their quality and their results. Ideally, such a process owner should be high up in the organization and should have support within the organization.

Carrying out process management means regularly checking to see if the processes comply with the objectives (i.e., effectiveness) and whether they do so in the best possible way (i.e., efficiency). To establish this, the objectives of the processes must first be made explicit. It also requires feedback from the processes. This means that *key performance indicators* (KPIs) must be defined. The KPIs indicate at what level of performance the processes are run. After the KPIs have been defined, the next step is to measure them. Repeating the measurements periodically makes it possible to discern any improvements in the processes. It is also possible to set certain targets for the processes— and to compare the measurement results against these targets.

The exact objectives being strived for and the corresponding KPIs depend, in part, on the situation. It is possible, however, to provide a number of important general KPIs. These can be specified in more detail for an individual organization.

Strategic Dialogue

The goal of the Strategic Dialogue is a consistent and achievable set of business objectives to which all IT activities are related. This provides IT developments with a focus. The objective gives rise to the KPIs shown in Exhibit 8.2.

EXHIBIT 8.2 KPIs of Strategic Dialogue	
Effectiveness	**Efficiency**
• Percentage of business objectives achieved.	• Frequency and duration of determining business cases.
• Percentage of projects producing desired results.	• Average duration of elaborating business cases.
• Percentage of projects stopped prematurely.	• Average duration of decision taking at first and second levels of approval.
• Average time required to respond to internal or external impulses.	

Each of these KPIs gives an indication of the effectiveness or efficiency of the Strategic Dialogue. The percentage of projects that is stopped prematurely, for example, indicates how carefully projects are started. The Strategic Dialogue ensures that projects are only started if they contribute to an acknowledged business objective and have a positive business case. This decreases the chances of projects being stopped prematurely because they fail to produce the expected results or because there was an unexpected resource problem.

The frequency and duration of determining the business cases to be elaborated is a KPI that says something about the efficiency of the process. If the organization has a good overview and has set up an efficient mechanism to keep a finger on the pulse, the necessary discussions can be carried out regularly—and kept short. The other KPIs mentioned above also say something about the efficiency of the Strategic Dialogue.

Architectural Services

The purpose of the Architectural Services process is to create frameworks, guidelines, and tools that result in IT solutions, with a high anticipatory content, that fit into the information system as a whole.

The related KPIs are shown in Exhibit 8.3.

EXHIBIT 8.3 KPIs of Architectural Services

Effectiveness	Efficiency
• Ratio of defensive/offensive projects, anticipative projects, and "irregular" projects (projects not carried out according to any strategy). • Satisfaction about project results two years after implementation, classified by strategy (defensive/offensive, anticipative, or no strategy). • Duration of projects (from receiving the assignment to elaborating the business case, up to and including implementation) classified by strategy • Cost of projects (from receiving the assignment to elaborating the business case, up to and including implementation) classified by strategy.	• Average time spent drawing up a project-start architecture. • Average time spent issuing a building permit. • Average time spent drawing up the architectures for business cases. • Average number of adjustments to the project-start architecture.

According to the exhibit, the effectiveness of the Architectural Services process can be derived from the percentages of defensive/offensive projects, anticipative projects, and "irregular" projects that have not been carried out according to any strategy: The more successful Architectural Services is, the higher the percentage of anticipative projects and the lower the number of irregular projects. Also, if the concept of enterprise architecture is dealt with properly, the average duration of anticipative projects will shorten, as use can be made increasingly of the already implemented architecture. As more work is carried out according to the architecture, lasting satisfaction with the IT solutions should increase and development costs should drop.

Efficiency is measured, among other things, by the speed with which enterprise architectures and project-start architectures are set up and building permits are issued. The care with which this is done (the number of required adjustments afterward) is also indicative of an efficient process.

Development with Architecture

The Development with Architecture process is intended to create IT solutions with a high anticipatory content that fit in with the information system as a whole.

The KPIs for Development with Architecture are shown in Exhibit 8.4.

EXHIBIT 8.4 KPIs of Development with Architecture	
Effectiveness	**Efficiency**
• Satisfaction with the project result of the anticipative projects after two years. • Average time spent on making adjustments in applications, classified by strategy. • Percentage of maintenance effort resulting from adjustments in other applications. • Percentage of building permits that are refused. • Percentage of building permits that are revoked.	• Degree to which standards and templates are used. • Number of coordination sessions with other projects.

The anticipative strategy strives to produce an IT solution that is prepared for the future, whatever that future may look like. Whether this has been achieved, can only be seen from the degree of satisfaction with the IT solution after two years. The percentage of maintenance effort resulting from adjustments to other applications is an indication of the anticipatory content of the IT solution. If adjustments have many side-effects in other applications, the ability to change and hence the anticipatory content are relatively small. The average time it takes to make adjustments, classified by strategy, gives another indication of the success of Development with Architecture. If building permits are frequently refused or revoked, there is definitely something wrong with the effectiveness of Development with Architecture.

The use of standards and templates is an indication of the efficiency of the development process: Standards and templates provide for at the same time rapid and high-quality procedures. The number of coordination sessions with other projects also says something about the efficiency of the process: If the project-start architecture works well, very little coordination with other projects is necessary and the number of coordination sessions will drop.

Development without Architecture

The Development without Architecture process is intended to create IT solutions rapidly under the extreme pressure of time, but in a highly controlled way. This objective leads to the KPIs shown in Exhibit 8.5.

EXHIBIT 8.5 KPIs of Development without Architecture	
Effectiveness	**Efficiency**
• Percentage of defensive/ offensive projects that are finished at the agreed time.	• Average time taken to decide on defensive/offensive strategy.
• Percentage of defensive/ offensive projects that are accompanied by an anticipative strategy	• Moment during the process when it is decided to opt for a parallel anticipative strategy.
• Percentage of temporary solutions that are actually removed after two years.	• Average effort necessary to remove temporary solutions.

If the Development without Architecture process is effective, the majority of defensive/offensive projects will be accompanied by an anticipative project. The result of the defensive/offensive projects will be produced at the time agreed and most of the project results will have been replaced by a structural solution two years later.

One of the indicators that show that the process is efficient is that temporary solutions can be removed without much effort because efficiency was taken into account from the start. In addition, efficiency is, to a great extent, determined by the speed at which decisions are made.

As stated, KPIs can be provided with targets. If one or more defined KPIs fails to meet the targets that have been set, the cause of this must be sought.

Targets differ per organization, depending, among other things, on the level of ambition of the organization. For example, an organization may strive to achieve a percentage of anticipative projects of 80% within a period of three years. The target at the end of the first year is 30%, after two years 60%, and, after three years, 80%. If the target is not reached, the reason for this must be identified. It may be that the organization is under extreme time pressure, that the anticipative strategy does not run smoothly, or the organization resorts to a defensive/offensive strategy too easily. When the cause is known, measures can be taken.

A frequently used tool for defining KPIs, and relating them to objectives, is the Balanced Score Card.[2]

How to deal with KPIs is illustrated in the fictitious example below. In this example, measurements are taken every year to see the desired effect of working according to DYA.

The first step is to measure the achieved business objectives. To achieve business objectives, projects are started. In most cases, there are several projects to realize a single business objective. This is shown in Exhibit A.

EXHIBIT A	Achieved Business Objectives	
	Number of Business Objectives Set	**Number of Business Objectives Realized**	**Number of Projects**
2002	21	13	122
2003	19	14	110
2004	23	20	76

Exhibit B shows that the percentage of business objectives achieved is increasing.

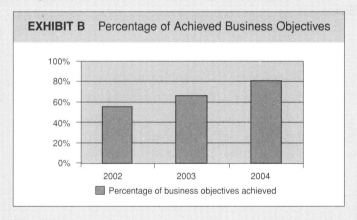

EXHIBIT B Percentage of Achieved Business Objectives

Percentage of business objectives achieved

The question now is whether there is a relationship with working under architecture according to DYA. In other words, has the number of projects that run according to the anticipative strategy increased? Exhibit C shows according to which development strategy projects were carried out.

EXHIBIT C	Projects and Strategies			
	Anticipative	**Offensive**	**Defensive**	**"Irregular"**	**Total**
2002	13	17	22	70	122
2003	50	11	16	33	110
2004	55	7	6	8	76

Exhibit D shows that the percentage of projects carried out according to the anticipative strategy is increasing.

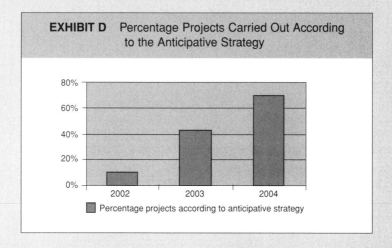

EXHIBIT D Percentage Projects Carried Out According to the Anticipative Strategy

Exhibit E shows the positive correlation between working according to DYA and the extent to which business objectives are achieved.

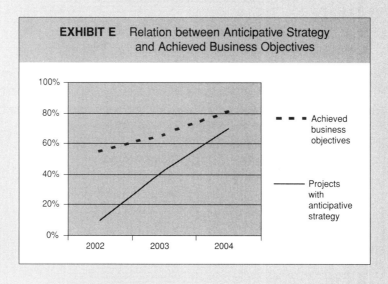

EXHIBIT E Relation between Anticipative Strategy and Achieved Business Objectives

GOVERNANCE: COHERENCE AND AGILITY

Governance is indispensable for enabling the processes of Strategic Dialogue, Architectural Services, and Development with(out) Architecture to run smoothly and to guarantee that they contribute toward achieving the business objectives. Governance is about responsibilities, coordination, monitoring, and maintenance of processes. Governance is the last piece of the puzzle in achieving coherence and agility.

Coherence is achieved because top management provides the organization with a focus in concrete business objectives and a clear interpretation of the first level of the architectural framework. Coherence is also achieved by good coordination by the project portfolio team.

Agility is achieved by placing responsibility at the lowest possible level in the organization. The frameworks are kept to a bare minimum, within which employees can move freely. Agility is also achieved by assigning clear responsibilities, so that it is known who decides what and a decision vacuum is avoided. Finally, agility is achieved by having clear procedures, with projects knowing what is expected of them and when.

INTERMEZZO: EMBEDDING DYNAMIC ARCHITECTURE AT TELEBEL

Switching to the concept of dynamic architecture, TeleBel has decided to hold on to existing procedures as much as possible so as to allow the switch to be as smooth as possible. Exhibit 8.6 outlines the main steps of TeleBel's current procedures.

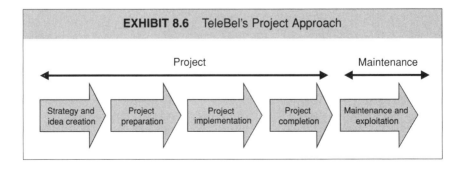

EXHIBIT 8.6 TeleBel's Project Approach

Strategy and the creation of ideas constitute a process in which TeleBel investigates what long-term business choices the company will make. In addition, ideas to realize these choices are generated and reviewed for feasibility. This process is completed by identifying the ideas that are worth elaborating in detail.

The second step is what is referred to inside TeleBel as project preparation. This process consists of elaborating the ideas generated in the previous step. During this step, the contours of the solution are defined, and feasibility and financial consequences are investigated. The last step consists of writing a project plan.

During the project implementation phase, the project is realized in accordance with the project plan. The proposed solution is created and implemented.

In the project completion phase, the results produced are handed over to maintenance and exploitation. This phase also includes providing and receiving feedback on what went well in the project and what should be improved.

Maintenance and usage ensure that the proposed solution is kept operational and minor maintenance is carried out.

The main problem within TeleBel is that there is no overview of what the projects will achieve, or which business processes, applications, and infrastructure are present at any one time. Each of the projects individually investigates the relationships with other projects. TeleBel's management has found that at least 30% of all project budgets is spent on coordination with other projects. This affects agility and, for that reason, business management is starting to complain about deteriorating time-to-market. Management believes that projects are leading their own lives and ambition levels are being raised. An example is the introduction of new technology during the project implementation phase.

Partly as a result of these problems, management has decided to work according to the concept of dynamic enterprise architecture. In order to relieve the organization as much as possible, there has been a request not to throw existing procedures overboard entirely.

After some research, the model represented in Exhibit 8.7 emerged.

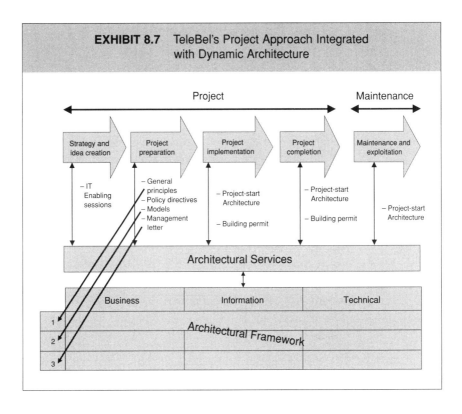

EXHIBIT 8.7 TeleBel's Project Approach Integrated with Dynamic Architecture

An Architectural Services process is set up within TeleBel. The relationships between this process and the company's existing procedures are established. The aim of establishing these relationships is to identify the points in the overall procedure where the Architectural Services process must be embedded. The aim of setting up the Architectural Services process is twofold:

1. Guaranteeing the cohesion between all more or less independent projects.
2. Creating clarity, at the earliest possible stage, in the architecture of the solution that must be achieved in a project.

To achieve these goals, the following measures were agreed:

- All known principles and policy directives that are applied, either explicitly or implicitly, will be collected, classified, and published by the architects.

- If the need arises for new or different principles and policy directives, this must be apparent from new projects. Whenever appropriate, new principles and policy directives will come into force. These must be approved by TeleBel management.

- Architectural models will be created during project preparations.

- After the project preparations, not only will the budget and planning be approved (as was already the case in the past), but also the architecture of the solution. If this is the case, a building permit will be issued for the project. During the implementation of the project, this building permit will be tested regularly by the architect responsible.

- The project-start architecture will be introduced to provide for the handover from architecture to project. This project-start architecture defines the context of the solution, based on the models that have already been created during project preparation.

- The project-start architecture will be evaluated and adjusted, if necessary, at the end of the project. Afterward it will be handed over to maintenance and exploitation.

- The building permit will also be evaluated during the completion of the project. If it turns out that the project deviated from the project-start architecture, without a good reason for doing so, the building permit can still be revoked.

- Thinking in terms of development strategies will be implemented. If the defensive or offensive strategy is chosen, it is compulsory to make arrangements during project preparation for the anticipative strategy and to record this in a management letter.

- To bring business and IT closer together, an IT-enabling session will be introduced in the strategy- and idea-creation phase. This means an agreement to have quarterly sessions, in which business presents its plans and IT indicates which IT trends would be appropriate. Together, they can then specify the business objectives in more detail and identify the IT enablers.

Notes

1. W.F.G. Mastenbroek. *Verandermanagement* [Change Management] (Heemstede, NL: Holland Business Publications, 1997).
2. R.S. Kaplan and D.P. Norton, *The Balanced Scorecard: Translating Strategy into Action* (Boston: Harvard Business School, 1996).

CONCLUSION

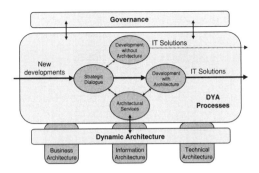

Information technology has high potential. We can see evidence of IT's potential around us everywhere. Today it is almost easier to buy a book from abroad than at the bookshop around the corner. We work just as easily at home as we do at the office. Exchanging information is a piece of cake, so are creating new forms of chain integration and removing borders between organizations.

However, it is not always easy to use this potential to the fullest. Evidence of that can also be seen around us everywhere. The Christmas shopping ordered online is not always delivered on time. Private bank account data can sometimes be viewed by strangers. And, in the meantime, IT management and maintenance costs are rising sky high.

The demands placed on IT today are, therefore, great. Everything has to be fast, faster, the fastest—otherwise the competition gets there first. Clients notice that immediately. Yet, at the same time, coherence in the supply of information has never been as important as it is today. We need to engage in flexible partnerships, to have many sales channels instead of one—and we need to facilitate the client who gets to be deeply involved in our business processes.

The challenge that modern organizations face is to find a balance between the simultaneous demands for agility and for coherence. In this book, we have described one way to meet this challenge. We did so by adding speed to development with architecture. We call this *dynamic architecture.*

There are two sides to dynamic architecture: the content side and the process side. Architecture is dynamic in content if it has been designed in such a way that adaptation to new and often unforeseen developments can be carried out quickly and economically. A great deal has already been written about the content side of architecture.

In this book, we focused on the process side of architecture: how to deal with architecture. We are convinced that the critical success factor for working under architecture is the way in which architecture is dealt with.

We expressed our vision in ten principles:

1. Architecture is strategic if IT is strategic.

2. Architecture must facilitate speed of change.

3. Communication between business and IT management is crucial.

4. Business objectives govern the development of architecture.

5. The level of architecture will be continually raised if architecture is aligned to important business changes.

6. Architecture must be developed "just enough, just in time."

7. Working under architecture is supported by a theoretical and working model.

8. Transparent relations must be defined.

9. Several development strategies are distinguished.

10. Architectural principles and processes must be an integral part of the organization.

We gave shape to these principles in the DYA model's three processes. In the *Strategic Dialogue*, business cases are used to determine which business objectives the organization strives for and which projects are used to achieve these objectives. *Architectural Services* is the process in which architectures are set up and made available to the business case teams and project teams. In the *Development with(out) Architecture* process, IT solutions are created. Exhibit 9.1 shows the processes of the DYA model.

Our approach differs in a number of crucial ways from more traditional architectural methods:

- Contrary to the traditional project-based approach, with a planning horizon of a few years, in the Architectural Services

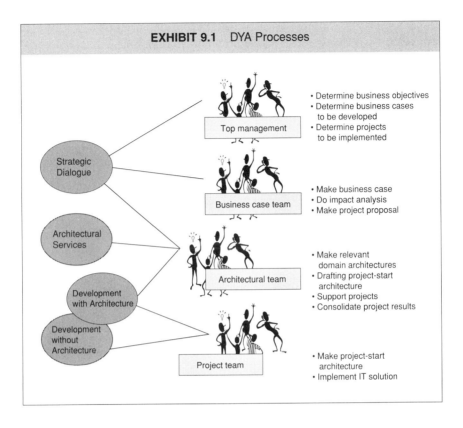

EXHIBIT 9.1 DYA Processes

process we present a continuous, cyclical, just-enough, just-in-time process.

- With the Strategic Dialogue tools, we bridge the traditional gap between business and IT.

- In contrast to the companywide architecture that is drawn up for the organization in one go, we propose a just-enough, just-in-time approach, creating only those domain architectures that are needed at the time.

- Contrary to architecture as a separate activity, which runs more or less alongside the organization, we propose an architectural process that is fully embedded in the organization's change processes.

- We curtail the unbridled phenomenon of bypassing architecture on all sides by providing a delineated space for development without architecture when such development is needed under special circumstances (e.g., time pressures).

If your organization uses architecture in the way described in this book, you will see that both coherence and agility thrive—and that it is possible to increase both coherence and agility in balance with each other. This enables your organization to make optimal use of IT's ever-increasing potential.

APPENDICES

APPENDIX A

Technique for Interactive Process Design

INTRODUCTION

The Technique for Interactive Process Design (TIPD) is a method used to analyze business processes and the associated use of information within an organization. It is an interactive approach, in which those who carry out the process play a key role.

As its name implies, TIPD is an interactive process. It involves holding sessions in which employees, interacting with each other, map out the various business processes. The underlying principle here is that the employees "do the work" themselves even as they are guided by a process supervisor.

When the process is mapped out, bottlenecks are identified. These are noted, classified according to various perspectives, and then linked to possible solutions.

First, employees identify the extent that the present supply of information supports the business processes of the organization and the demands and desires that will apply to the future information supply. Inviting one or more technical specialists to participate guarantees that the eventual requirements are feasible.

Then, upper management adapts this set of demands and wishes—or adds new demands. The latter usually occurs from a different line of approach, for example, from a future perspective.

Working with TIPD has the following advantages:

- Short lead times
- Minimal demand on employee time
- Immediate consensus among all parties (users and IT)
- Immediate overview of bottlenecks
- Immediate feedback to those involved

FIVE STEPS OF TIPD

Within TIPD there are five distinct steps:

1. *Preliminary Discussion with the Client*

This discussion aims to identify the business objective to be achieved. It is also used to establish availability of employees. It is important that the entire process to be investigated is covered by the team members.

2. *Introductory Meeting*

The main aim of this meeting is to determine exactly which processes are concerned, what the beginnings and ends of the processes will be, and whether the appropriate people are present. The participants are asked to collect all forms that are used in the processes in question and to bring these along to the next session.

3. *Feedback to the Client*

The objective of this consultation is to verify the results of the introductory meeting and to assess the attitude within the organization.

This example concerns an organization that wanted to have the functionality of its Help Desk investigated. During the introductory meeting, the
processes in Exhibit A emerged.

EXHIBIT A   Processes

Process	Start	Finish
Registration	Request via telephone, oral, or written service request	Message entered into the system
Delegation	Report from the Helpdesk (1st line) to the 2nd line	Feedback to the Helpdesk (1st line)
Software deliverance	Request (by internal or external organization)	Signature
Problem analysis	Problem report	Problem solved or delegated

4. *The Actual TIPD Session*

The participants sit around a table, on which there is a large board. The
participants have small magnetic symbols, representing the elements of
detailed process flowcharts as created within the Administrative
Organization. The process is mapped out on the board in mutual agreement. The processes and subprocesses were already identified in the
introductory meeting.

In addition to the participants, each TIPD session has two supervising
roles. The first is the *moderator,* who ensures that the entire process runs
smoothly. The *scribe* takes minutes, ensuring that discussions are recorded
accurately. It is useful to have a systems designer perform the role of
scribe. This person can record the results in such a way that it provides the
right input for the next step in the process, which is the systems design.
In addition, this person, having experienced the entire process, can easily switch to the next stage (unlike the well-known process of "throwing it
over the fence"). This guarantees continuity into the next stage.

As a result, all parties involved are aware of the demands and wishes, the origins are known, there is universal support for them, and we know that they are feasible.

Part of the help desk process is shown in Exhibit A.1.

When a form is used within the process, whether electronic or printed, the person responsible supplies a sample of the completed

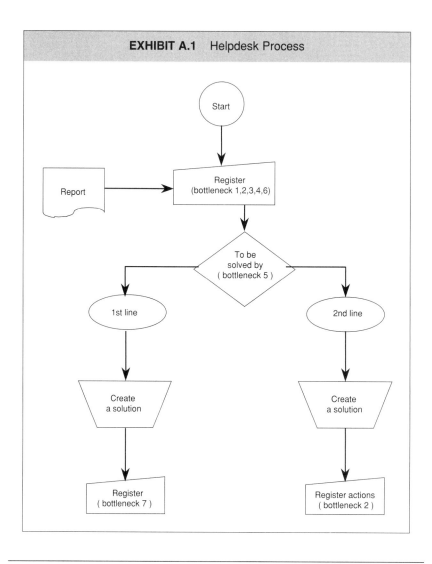

EXHIBIT A.1   Helpdesk Process

form in question. This is numbered, both on the form and on the small magnetic symbol representing the form, and then archived.

As soon as a bottleneck is identified, the person who presented it writes the issue on a card, which is then attached to the board. This card states the initials of the person concerned and the bottleneck sequence number. This number is also copied onto the magnetic symbol of the activity. This makes it easier to determine at a later stage who identified the bottleneck and in what context. This is done for all processes from start to finish. Having completed this stage, participants take another look at the bottlenecks found and try to decide whether all bottlenecks have been identified. If not, any missing ones will be added.

The participants then classify the processes at a higher level of abstraction, which we refer to as core functions.

The bottlenecks are then linked to those core functions.

Exhibit A.2 shows the bottlenecks classified by core function.

EXHIBIT A.2 Process Bottlenecks	
(Description)	**Person**
5 Route: Helpdesk	
There is no standard list of departments/persons who take certain messages. For that reason, it is difficult to determine who to send the message to.	M T
6 No standard problem description available in the registration system: Helpdesk	M T
As there is no standard description of messages, identical messages are not recognized as such because a different description has been used the second time. This makes it difficult to retrieve previous solutions (see also bottleneck 7).	
7 No standard description of solutions available in the registration system: Helpdesk	H G
As a standard description of solutions does not exist, a solution that is the same as one applied earlier, is not recognized as such because a different description has been used. This prevents insight into the solutions that can be used for particular types of messages.	

Participants are then asked to write on cards which possibilities are offered by the present information system. These cards are divided into groups and assigned to the respective functions. Then, participants step back and focus on the more distant future, for example by watching a video showing a state-of-the-art company either in their own field or in a different one. On the basis of the process, the bottlenecks, the degree of support from the present information system, and the possibilities for the distant future, the participants define for each core function the relevant demands and wishes for the future supply of information. Solutions are defined for each individual bottleneck. The first process is dealt with in full, during a plenary session, to show how it is done. The remaining processes are dealt with in smaller groups. When all require-ments have been defined, their priority is indicated by means of stick-ers. This is done for each core function. For this stage, use can be made of the MoSCoW principle discussed in Chapter 7.

5. Decision-Making Process by Management

One or more of the participants in the TIPD session inform Man-agement of their results. Afterward, Management may add demands and wishes and/or change the priorities based on their perspectives. To conclude, Management decides on the demands and wishes to be met.

Solutions for selected bottlenecks, which were accepted during the decision-making meeting, can be found in Exhibits A.3, A.4, and A.5.

EXHIBIT A.3 Solution for Bottleneck 5	
Subject	**Route: Bottleneck 5**
Description	A delegation matrix needs to be drawn up. This is a synonym for Owners' matrix.
Remarks	A matrix has a limiting effect. This means that the matrix must have a coverage of 100% and that there must be a 2nd line available for each product, including "someone else" (in principle, the head of IC). The matrix must clearly state what *should* and *should not* be done.

EXHIBIT A.4 Solution for Bottleneck 6

Subject	Standard Problem Description: Bottleneck 6
Description	Problems must be given standard descriptions in order to be easily recognized and retrieved.
Remarks	Do not use "problem" as a term anymore. Use the term "message"—in this case, "message description." A growth model should be created and managed for these standards, enabling new products and synonyms to be included immediately Responsible: Head of IC

EXHIBIT A.5 Solution for Bottleneck 7

Subject	Standard Solution Description: Bottleneck 7
Description	Solutions must be given standard descriptions to be easily recognized and retrieved. These descriptions can be created and implemented at a later stage.
Remarks	The knowledge bank should not lead to automatic behaviors and passivity. Routine tasks, however, are possible.

APPENDIX B

Information Economics

Information Economics (IE) is a method of assessing investments in IT, both in quantitative and qualitative terms. For a full description of this method, see Parker and Benson's *Information Economics*.[1]

Within IE, projects are assessed on 10 criteria before they start up. These criteria are subsequently weighed to arrive at a score for each project. Exhibit B.1 summarizes criteria and method.

Exhibit B.2 gives a brief description of the assessment factors.

EXHIBIT B.1   IE Assessment Scheme

Assess-ment factor	Business Process Domain						Technology Domain						
	B1	B2	B3	B4	B5	B6	T1	T2	T3	T4			
	ROI	SM	CA	MI	CR	OR	SA	DU	TU	IR			
Weighting factor													
Influence +/−	+	+	+	+	+	−	+	−	−	−			
Projects	Appreciation									Score +	Score −	Score T
P1												
P2												

217

EXHIBIT B.2	IE Assessment Factors		
Assessment Factor	**Abbre-viation**	**Name**	**Meaning**
B1	ROI	Return on Investment	The degree to which the investment can be recovered.
B2	SM	Strategic Match	The degree to which the project is related to the strategic aims.
B3	CA	Competitive Advantage	The degree of advantage that the project provides with regard to competitors.
B4	MI	Management Information	The degree to which the project (potentially) provides management information about core activities.
B5	CR	Competitive Response	The degree to which the company incurs competitive disadvantages by not carrying out the project.
B6	OR	Project or Organiza-tional Risk	The degree to which the company is capable of carrying out the changes connected with this project.
T1	SA	Strategic IS Architecture	The degree to which the project matches the IS strategy.
T2	DU	Definitional Uncertainty	The degree to which the project requirements can be specified accurately.
T3	TU	Technical Uncertainty	The degree to which the required technical knowledge and skills for the project are available.
T4	IR	Infrastructural Risk	The degree to which the project demands nonproject-related investments in infra-structure (e.g., DBMS).

EXHIBIT B.3 IE Assessment Factors Form

Circle the figure that applies best to the project.

B2	Project has no relationship with strategic aims.	0	1	2	3	4	5	Project is fully related to strategic aims.
B3	Project provides no competitive edge.	0	1	2	3	4	5	Project provides a great deal o competitive edge.
B4	Project has no relationship to management information.	0	1	2	3	4	5	Project is essential for producing management information about core activities.
B5	Not carrying out the project provides no competitive disadvantage; the project could easily be postponed for 12 months.	0	1	2	3	4	5	Failure to carry out the project leads to a great competitive disadvantage, the project must not be postponed at any cost.
B6	An implementation plan exists. Processes and procedures have been documented.	0	1	2	3	4	5	No implementation plan exists. Processes and procedures have not been documented.
T1	The project has no relationship to IT policies.	0	1	2	3	4	5	The project is an integral part of IT policies, and supports other projects.
T2	Project requirements are known in detail and have been approved, the scope is known, little change to be expected.	0	1	2	3	4	5	Project requirements are unknown and difficult to describe, the scope is unknown, many changes to be expected.
T3	Technical knowledge and skills are present, training is not necessary.	0	1	2	3	4	5	Technical knowledge and skills are not present, training necessary.
T4	The project uses existing technical infrastructure.	0	1	2	3	4	5	The project uses a completely new technical infrastructure.

IE works as follows. Weighing factors are established first, after which an assessment can be carried out for each project using these weighing factors. Weighing factors express the relative weight or importance of each of the assessment factors.

For each project, a score between 0 and 5 is assigned to each assessment factor. The form shown in Exhibit B.3 serves as an aid to identify these factors.

Multiplying the assigned value for each assessment factor by the weighing factor, one obtains a total value for each assessment factor. Adding up all "+ factors" leads to the "+ score," which is the positive score that indicates the strategic need for the project. Adding up all "– factors" leads to the "– score," which stands for the negative score, or the risks involved in the project. Finally, a T-score, or total score, can be calculated for each project. Exhibit B.4 can be used to assess the investment proposals for each project.

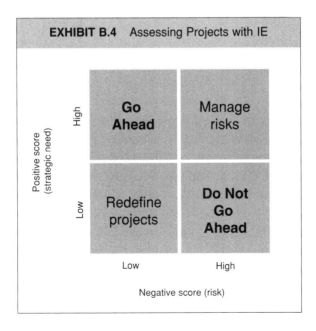

EXHIBIT B.4 Assessing Projects with IE

220

Standards can be defined beforehand for the risk that an organization is willing to run (negative score) and the strategic need (positive score). If a project exceeds both standards, this indicates an extreme strategic need—but, at the same time, a high risk as well. If the organization wishes to go ahead with the project in such a situation, it will be necessary to control the risks.

Notes

1. M. M. Parker, and R. J. Benson, *Information Economics* (Englewood Cliffs, NJ: Prentice Hall, 1988).

APPENDIX C

Architecture Maturity Model and Dynamic Architecture

ARCHITECTURE MATURITY MODEL

The Architecture Maturity Model (AMM) is a model used to determine the position of the organization in areas of architecture and the steps that should be taken on the road to further professionalization. AMM was set up by analogy with CMM (Capability Maturity Model). What CMM is for software engineering, AMM is for architecture. AMM can be used to determine and increase the degree of maturity of thinking about and working with architecture in an organization. The model distinguishes five levels of maturity. Depending on the level that an organization is at and the level which it strives to achieve, steps can be distinguished in order to further professionalize the role of architecture.

Exhibit C.1 shows, in a slightly adapted form derived from the Nolan Norton Institute,[1] the five levels of AMM on the basis of the aspects of management, definition, role of architect, processes and products. A more extensive description of AMM can be found in various META Group documents.

EXHIBIT C.1 AMM Levels

	Management	Definitions	Role of Architect	Process	Products
Level 1: Initial	No control	Careful first attempts	Not assigned	Not present	Rough idea
Level 2: Repeatable	Control over persons	Established but still being discussed	Assigned	Roughly described per domain	Uniformly described per domain
Level 3: Defined	Control over the process	Established and accepted	Responsible for the process	Attuned between domains	Uniformly described and standardized over domains
Level 4: Managed	Control over the results	Established and accepted	Responsible for the results	Integrated process	Centrally coordinated
Level 5: Optimizing	Control over continuous improvement	Established and accepted	Initiates innovation and improvements	Optimized process	Continually adapted

On level 1, activities in the field of architecture are undertaken, but these are ad hoc and are completely dependent on the initiatives taken by the IT professionals from their personal conviction as to the value of architecture. The role of architect is not recognized within the organization.

On level 2, employees have been assigned the role of architect, and with it the responsibility of providing architectural products. The activities in the field of architecture occur in isolation, per department, domain, or project. A start has been made with the description of products, processes and definitions; however, because these are created from different perspectives, they still contain inconsistencies.

On level 3, the various architectural activities are better attuned to each other. Standards have been defined, agreement has been reached on terminology, and products and processes have been described. The architectural process has become repeatable. The architect is responsible for the architectural process and has an influence on the development process.

Where on level 3 the different architectural initiatives are integrated into a single coordinated process, on level 4 the switch has been made towards architectural activities that arise from a single overall vision throughout the organization. The architect is responsible for the results of the architectural process and is directed by those results. All development projects are carried out under architecture.

Level 5 is the level of continuous improvement and innovation. This is what the architect focuses on.

META Group indicates that in 2004, 75% of architecture processes in the Global 2000 were on level 2 or lower. It is expected that this percentage will be reduced to 55% by 2007.[2]

AMM AND DYA

The AMM can be used well in combination with DYA to further professionalize the architectural thinking and working in the organization. The vision that constitutes the basis of DYA is a vision that matches AMM levels 4 and 5: the purposiveness, the strategic character of architecture, the embedding of architectural principles and processes in the organization, and the involvement of top management. The DYA concept can, therefore, be used to achieve higher AMM levels. Depending on the AMM level of the organization, the emphasis will be on different parts of DYA.

It all starts with establishing at which AMM level the organization is. This can be carried out with the help of an AMM assessment. By now, various methods have been developed that can be used to carry out such an assessment. Depending on the organization's level, it is then decided what steps should be taken next.

From Level 1 to Level 2

At level 1, architecture is more or less the hobby of a few fanatics. They get the chance to carry out small pilot projects, which show a certain degree of success. The challenge at this level is to get architecture away from the realm of ad hoc decisions and present it as a proper way of working. The first to convince is the organization's IT management. The prospective architect should generate awareness. This is a good moment to bring the DYA concept to the attention of the IT management. Present them with this book and provide presentations.

From Level 2 to Level 3

The challenge at level 2 is to get architecture away from the individual (often IT) domains, to lift it to a higher, more general level. The first priority is to involve the business in the thinking in architectural terms. In this phase, it is important to present architecture as an enabler instead of as a hindrance. Thinking in development strategies should receive ample attention, as well as the business-goal-oriented nature of the architectural processes.

In addition, cohesion among the various architecture initiatives should be increased. The architectural framework can serve as an aid here, as it can be used to assign to each initiative a place in relation to the other initiatives. The division into three levels is especially useful in obtaining cohesion. Relating all initiatives to statements at level one or two of the framework clarifies their interrelationship.

An organization at this level is also ready to set up business case teams for carrying out business projects. In addition, development under architecture will take more shape by introduction of the project-start architecture.

A risk with the transition from level 2 to 3 is that the architectural processes are perceived as too "monolithical." It may look too much like bureaucratic processes being set up, the advantages of which for the business are unclear. Architecture thus becomes a burden. This can be prevented or remedied by using the DYA approach of Architectural Services.

From Level 3 to Level 4

Moving from level 3 to level 4 demands a change toward a comprehensive vision, supported by top management. The primarily bottom-up approach must be complemented by top-down commitment and focus. The issue is now to involve top management. This starts by convincing top management of the usefulness of architecture for the organization. Subsequently, top management should realize that their input and involvement with architecture is indispensable. Top management should become aware of the importance of architecture.

This can be achieved by referring to previously achieved successes (e.g., cost savings, shorter time-to-market, or opportunities seized). The importance of IT for the organization should also be stressed. The increase in the role of IT over the last few years has been a stealthy process and awareness of this greater role has lagged behind. The organization's dependency on IT can be demonstrated with a few simple examples. Once top management is convinced of the strategic importance of IT, it will be more inclined to adopt a structural approach to IT.

The involvement of top management can be obtained by using the three levels from the architectural framework. By showing that the statements on level one of the framework are the responsibility of top management, and subsequently relating these statements to domain-specific architectural implementations, it will be made clear that top management is responsible—and for the specialist implementations at the lowest level.

Just like with business management, any fear that top management may have for bureaucracy can be removed by emphasizing the development strategies and the target-oriented approach of DYA.

EXHIBIT C.2 AMM and DYA	
AMM Level	**Emphasis on**
Level 1: Initial	• Creating awareness among IT management—draw attention to the importance of architecture.
Level 2: Repeatable	• Involving business—attention for thinking in terms of development strategies and target-oriented nature of architecture. • Introducing cohesion into architectural initiatives with the aid of the architectural framework. • Introducing business case teams.
Level 3: Defined	• Involving top management and making top managers responsible for working under architecture—indicating the strategic importance of IT and, hence, the importance of architecture. • Putting level 1 of the architectural framework with top management. • Introducing joint IT enabling sessions.
Level 4: Managed	• Implementing Strategic Dialogue between business and IT top management as a continuous process.
Level 5: Optimizing	• Embedding Strategic Dialogue, Architectural Services, and Development with and without Architecture as continuous processes of innovation and improvement.

This is also the moment the joint IT enabling sessions of business and IT top management can be introduced. By having one or two workshops, top management can be made aware of the importance of their involvement and a first rudimentary vision can be developed.

From Level 4 to Level 5

On level 4, working under architecture has become a widely supported and implemented policy of the organization. To make the transition to level 5, it must be deeply embedded in the policy of the organization as a whole. This means implementation of the Strategic Dialogue: business and IT together determine which business objectives the organization wants to achieve and which IT solutions should be used for this. When the transition to level 5 has been made, it is followed by a process of continuous improvement of the Strategic Dialogue, Architectural Services, and Development with Architecture.

Depending on the level that an organization has reached, the emphasis will be on different elements of DYA. This has been summarized in Exhibit C.2.

Notes

1. Han Van Der Zee, Paul Laagland, Bas Hafkenscheid, and Leonie Geersing (Nolan Norton Institute), *Architectuur als Managementinstrument: Multi Client Study* [Architecture as a Management Instrument: A Multiclient Study] (The Hague: Ten Hagen & Stam, 2000).
2. Tim Westbrock, "Architecture Process Maturity Revisited and Revised" (Meta Group, May 2004); *www.eacommunity.com/articles.*

GLOSSARY

This section contains the definitions of the most important concepts used in the book.

Anticipative strategy   This strategy provides structural solutions with the capability to "anticipate" future business developments. Employing the anticipative strategy results in IT solutions that easily fit into the Architectural Framework. The anticipative strategy is implemented in the Development with Architecture process.

Architectural framework   This structure, in the form of a matrix, enables an architect to monitor and preserve consistency between the separate business initiatives that are constantly being launched within an organization. The framework also allows the architect to concentrate on specific components during the design process, while retaining an overall picture of the enterprise architecture as a whole.

   The Architectural Framework is divided into three high-level architectures (Business Architecture, Information Architecture, and Technical Architecture)—which are subdivided into domain architectures such as processes, data, and platforms—and three conceptual levels: general principles, policy directives, and models. The domain architectures make up the columns of the matrix, while the conceptual levels constitute the rows of the matrix.

Architectural principles   The general principles and policy directives that together form the foundation for developing an enterprise architecture (i.e., the first and second levels within the Architectural Framework).

Architectural Services   The process in which architectures are defined and made available to business case teams for use in the "Strategic Dialogue" process and to project teams for use in the "Development with Architecture" process.

Architectural team   The team within an organization responsible for carrying out the Architectural Services process.

Building permit   An instrument for measuring to what extent a project complies with the project-start architecture during the course of that project. Agreements made between the architect and the project team should be noted as an addendum to the building permit. If a project fails to comply with any of these agreements, its building permit can be withdrawn.

Business architecture   The architecture that sketches the organizational contours necessary to achieve the business objectives of the organization. Business architecture is concerned with three (architectural) objects: (1) the products and services that make it possible to achieve the business objectives; (2) the processes necessary to produce the products and services; and (3) the organizational structure of these processes.

Business case   One of the main products of the "Strategic Dialogue" process. A business case describes the general direction in which a solution should be sought, the expected impact of the solution, the consequences of implementing the solution, and a financial section.

Business objective   Organizations strive to achieve their business objectives. In order to make the objectives as clear as possible for the entire organization, they should be defined using SMART terms. *See* **SMART**.

Component-based development (CBD)   A system development method in which applications are broken down into components that are capable of operating independently of each other. Components should be designed to be easily replaceable and, where possible, reusable.

Conceptual levels   DYA discerns three distinct levels in defining architecture:
1. General principles
2. Policy directives
3. Models

These levels coincide with the rows in the Architectural Framework.

Defensive strategy This strategy contends with eventualities that threaten the continuity of an organization. The defensive strategy provides the organization with temporary solutions to counter these threats within a very short time span, and concentrates on solving the problem within the allotted time. These solutions are, therefore, said to have a high level of problem-solving content.

Development with Architecture This process provides structural IT solutions and achieves concrete business objectives, within the stated time frame, with the stated level of quality, and within acceptable costs.

Development without Architecture This DYA process provides temporary IT solutions, achieving concrete business objectives. The available time frame is, however, so short that concessions need to be made on costs, functionality, and quality.

Development strategy A predefined way of working that can be employed as the need or situation arises. Within DYA, three development strategies have been defined:

Anticipative

Defensive

Offensive

Domain architecture An architecture that has been designed for one particular type of object within an organization. Process architecture is an example of domain architecture. The columns in the Architectural Framework represent domain architectures.

DYA Dynamic Architecture for modeling and designing development. See also *Dynamic Architecture*

Dynamic Architecture An enterprise architecture that has been developed with speed of change in mind and, more specifically, the dynamics involved in facilitating change. These dynamics are built into the enterprise architecture and the processes that produce the enterprise architecture, thus allowing the enterprise architecture to *bend with the future* as this future unfolds and change almost simultaneously with developments in the market.

Dynamic process   The Architectural Services process is implemented as a dynamic process: At times of increasing or heavy workload, the architectural team is expanded; at times of decreasing or light workload, the number of members of the team is reduced.

Dynamic Systems Development Method (DSDM)   A development method that enhances the speed of development. Using time-boxing techniques and with a great deal of active participation of end users, the best result is reached in the shortest possible time frame.

e-business   Doing business electronically. "Business" in this definition entails the entire supply chain and is not restricted to just "front-office" operations. The demands and possibilities of e-business can result in the implementation of a complete new business model.

e-commerce   Doing business electronically, but restricted to "front-office" operations.

e-era   The period characterized by the emergence and increasing use of e-business. In this period, new demands have been placed on both the business and IT solutions. These demands are primarily for an increase in speed of change and an increase in consistency.

Enterprise architecture   A consistent set of rules and models that guides the design and implementation of processes, organizational structures, information flows, and technical infrastructure within an organization.

Environment model   The environment model is a diagram that details the areas of concern within which an IT solution is needed, and illustrates the business context within which the IT solution should function. The environment model is part of the project-start architecture and consists of a context diagram and a business process model of the organization.

eXtreme Programming   A development method aimed at speed of development. With the help of recursive techniques and active participation by the end user, the best possible result is reached in the shortest possible time frame.

First level of approval   The last step in the subprocess "Determine Business Cases." At this point, a decision is made as to which ideas will be worked out as business cases and the ones that will not.

General principles   The combined vision of business and IT management is reflected in the general principles. The general principles constitute the top level within the Architectural Framework. Providing the customer with a single point of contact for his or her enquiries is an example of a general principle.

Governance   The whole of organizational and procedural measures, the purpose of which is to coordinate activities in such a way that they make an optimum contribution to achieving the business objectives of the organization.

High anticipatory content   The capacity to be prepared for changes in the environment and thus respond quickly to these changes. Using the anticipative strategy results in an IT solution with a high anticipatory content.

High problem-solving content   The capacity to immediately resolve a problem, without taking future changes into consideration. Use of the defensive or offensive strategy results in an IT solution with a high problem-solving content.

Impact analysis   An impact analysis is a constituent part of a business case. If an organization decides to pursue a certain business objective, the resulting business case(s) must be elaborated by performing an analysis of the changes proposed in the business case and by predicting the expected impact of these changes on the organization as a whole.

Information architecture   The architecture that sketches the informational contours necessary to provide the organization with the information it requires. Information architecture is concerned with two (architectural) objects: (1) the information that is important for the proper functioning of the organization and (2) the applications that ensure that this information is distributed correctly within the organization.

Information Economics (IE)   A method to evaluate IT investments. IE is characterized by the balance between the quantitative aspects and the costs and returns related to quality.

Information planning   A method to summarize the required changes in the supply of information within an organization and to analyse and plan the consequences and impact of those changes. ISP (Information Strategy Planning) is an example of an information planning method.

IT enabler An IT development that makes a substantial contribution to attaining the main business objectives of an organization.

IT-enabling session An IT-enabling session is an instrument to establish which IT trends can be used by an organization to achieve its business objectives. Representatives of the various disciplines in business and IT participate in IT enabling sessions. Each session consists of one or more workshops held within a short time frame. In these workshops, a number of decisions are taken that lead to a priority list of business objectives, a priority list of IT enablers, and a selection of business objectives that can be worked out as a business case.

IT potential The full range of services that IT offers an organization, enabling the organization to seize opportunities as they arise or solve problems before they arise.

IT trend A new development in IT that is of increasing interest to the business community.

IT trend/business objective model An instrument to determine the relevancy of specific IT trends in relation to specific business objectives. Using this instrument, an organization gains insight into which trends can best be deployed as enablers.

Just-enough, just-in-time architecture Using this principle, architecture is developed as and when it is clear how and for what it will be used. Architecture development is, therefore, always linked to a business objective. This principle requires that the architectural team is flexible and that the number of architects, at a given moment, reflect the workload of the team.

Key performance indicator (KPI) An indicator for the level at which a process "performs." KPIs can be measured and compared with previously defined norm levels.

Level of architectural maturity The quality of the enterprise architecture and the architectural processes within an organization can be assessed objectively and expressed as a level of maturity. The level of maturity indicates to what extent the organization thinks and works in terms of architecture. It may give an indication of how and where the organization needs to improve to reach the next level of maturity.

Management letter   An instrument that explicitly defines the temporary nature of an IT solution that has been developed as a result of employing the defensive or offensive strategy. The management letter states clearly which course of action has been agreed upon to achieve the structural solution, as required by the anticipative strategy, and when this course of action will be implemented.

The management letter also contains the agreed-upon way in which money, functionality, and quality will be deployed to achieve the deadline set by the defensive or offensive strategy.

Models   Diagrams and descriptions of current and future (desirable) situations. Models constitute the third and lowest level in the Architectural Framework.

MoSCoW   MoSCoW is an acronym signifying the priority of system requirements:

- **M**ust have—Requirements that are essential for the system. If these requirements are not met, the system is unusable and worthless. Must haves are often defined as the "minimum usable subset" of system requirements.
- **S**hould have—Requirements that are important for the correct functioning of the system and would probably be defined as "must haves" if enough time was available to include them. They can, however, be left out.
- **C**ould have—Requirements that can easily be left out if the time available to complete a release of the system is insufficient.
- **W**ant to have but will not have this time around—Requirements that can be left out and can wait until the next round.

Next-minute architecture   Architecture as a collection of concrete guidelines for implementing new developments.

Offensive strategy   This strategy contends with (business) opportunities that appear suddenly. The offensive strategy provides the organization with a temporary solution to make the most of such an opportunity within a very short time and concentrates on creating the solution within the allotted time. These solutions are, therefore, said to have a high problem-solving content.

Policy directives General principles are translated into policy directives for each domain architecture. Policy directives make up the second level of the Architectural Framework. Standards and guidelines are examples of policy directives.

Project portfolio The total of business cases and projects being carried out at a given moment within an organization.

Project portfolio management The process of monitoring and managing the project portfolio on such aspects as status, choice of strategy, planning, and resources.

Project proposal One of the results of the Strategic Dialogue. A project proposal is the elaboration of a business case resulting in one or more concrete projects. A project proposal should contain the following aspects: project definition and assumptions; project organization; proposed approach, products, and planning; transfer, acceptance, implementation, and aftercare; resources; and maintenance and support.

Project-start architecture The enterprise architecture (general principles, policy directives, and models), as described in the Architectural Framework, is clarified or "translated" to meet the specific problems of a project. The project-start architecture delineates a concrete and usable framework within which the project should be carried out.

Second level of approval The last step in the process of "Strategic Dialogue." Based on the business case and project proposal, a decision is made whether the project should be carried out.

Service-oriented architecture Architectural concept within which business processes are subdivided into autonomous services. These services can be called upon where and when the service is needed, thus uncoupling the use of services and the services themselves and, thereby, achieving greater flexibility.

SMART An acronym signifying the requirements that every business objective formulation should meet:

Specific—the objective must be stated in concrete specific terms.

Measurable—it must be possible to measure when the objective has been reached.

Acceptable—the objective must be acceptable for the organization and the organization must be prepared to work to reach the objective.

Realistic—it must realistically be within the capability of the organization to reach the objective.

Time-bound—a time limit must be set within which the organization should reach its objective.

Strategic Benefiting the competitive position of the organization.

Strategic Dialogue The process that determines the business objectives, which are subsequently defined as business cases and further elaborated as concrete project proposals.

Strategic document A product of the "Determine Business Cases" sub-process. The strategic document contains a priority list of business objectives (including justification), a priority list of IT enablers (including justification), and a list of business cases needing further elaboration, including assumptions and restrictions such as maximum time, maximum costs, or minimum benefits.

Technical architecture The architecture that sketches the requirements for implementing the technical infrastructure of the organization. Technical architecture is concerned with three (architectural) objects: (1) the hardware, (2) network components, and (3) software (or middleware) to ensure that the applications can cooperate on information sharing.

Theoretical and working model The theoretical model illustrates the architectural concepts that make up DYA, while the working model demonstrates the practical application of these concepts.

Time-boxing A method to reach an objective by a certain date. Using time-boxing, deadlines are set by which certain objectives must be reached. Whatever happens, the deadline (date) remains the same. If it is threatened, the date will not be changed, but less functionality or quality will be delivered.

TIPD (Technique for Interactive Process Design)   A method for gathering and examining the business processes and the corresponding information requirements within an organization. This is an interactive approach, in which process workers and business experts play a key role.

Today architecture   Architecture as a description of the present situation.

Tomorrow architecture   Architecture as a blueprint for the desired, future situation.

BIBLIOGRAPHY

Ansoff, H.I. "Managing Surprise and Discontinuity: Strategic Response to Weak Signals." *Zeitschrift für betriebswirtschaftliche Forschung* 28 (1976): 129–152.

Boonstra, J.J. *Lopen Over Water* [Walking on Water]. Amsterdam: Vossiuspers, 2000.

Boreel, M., and P. Franken. *Gevangen Tussen Verleden en Toekomst* [Caught between Past and Present]. The Hague: Sogeti, 1998.

Butler Group. "Component-Based Development." Butler Group, 1998.

Cohen, L. *Quality Function Deployment: How to Make QFD Work for You.* Reading, MA: Addison-Wesley, 1995.

D' Souza, P.F., and A.C. Wills. *Objects, Components and Frameworks with ITIL: The Catalysis Approach.* Reading, MA: Addison-Wesley, 1998.

Dietz, J., P. Mallens, H. Goedvolk, and D. Rijsenbrij. "A Conceptual Framework for the Continuous Alignment of Business and ICT." Technische Universiteit Delft and Cap Gemini, December 1999.

DSDM Consortium. *Dynamic Systems Development Method*, ver. 3. Farnham, UK: Tesseract, 1997.

Gianotten, M.H.E., and J.J.H. Gianotten. *Digitaal Leiderschap* [Digital Leadership]. Giarte Media Group, May 1999.

Goedvolk, H. "Plaatsbepaling Informatie-architectuur" [Positioning Information Architecture]. Presentation at Euroforum Praktijkseminar

Informatie-architectuur [Euroforum Seminar Information Architecture]. Cap Gemini Institute, December 9, 1999.

Hamel, G., and C.K. Prahalad. *Competing for the Future*. Boston: Harvard Business School, 1996.

Hannigan, B. "Internet Infrastructure for eBusiness." Forrester Research, June 2000.

Harrison, R. "Understanding Your Organization's Character." *Harvard Business Review* 50 (May–June 1972): 119–128.

Hasper, W.J.J. *De Onderneming als Individualiteit* [The Enterprise as Individuality]. Alphen aan de Rijn, NL: Samsom, 1989.

Hauser, J.R., and D. Clausing. "The House of Quality." *Harvard Business Review* 66 (May–June 1988): 63–73.

Have, S. ten. "Gezond Verstand in Managementland" [Common Sense in Management Country]. *Nijenrode Management Review* 13 (March/April 1999): 56–65.

Heijden, T. van der, and J.J.H. Gianotten. *Trendrapport Topmanagement en IT 1999*. Giarte Research, August 1999.

Hertzberger, H. "De Ruimte van de Architect" [The Space of the Architect] [interviewed by Emile Bode]. *De Telegraaf* (October 9, 1999): T21.

Holland, C., H. Bouwman, and M. Smidts. "Back to the Bottom Line: Onderzoek naar Succesvolle e-Businessmodellen" [Back to the Bottom Line: Investigation of Successful e-Business Models]. ECP.NL, 2001.

Horn, L.A. ten. *Psychologische Aspecten van de Organisatie* [Psychological Aspects of the Organization]. Alphen aan den Rijn, NL: Samsom, 1994.

IT Trends Institute and Verkenningsinstituut Nieuwe Technologie/Sogeti. "Trends in IT: De Stand van 2001" [Trends in IT: The State of the Art in 2001]. Sogeti, January 2001.

Kaplan, R.S., and D.P. Norton. *The Balanced Scorecard: Translating Strategy into Action*. Boston: Harvard Business School, 1996.

Linthicum, D.S. *Enterprise Application Integration.* Reading, MA: Addison-Wesley, 1999.

Mastenbroek, W.F.G. *Verandermanagement.* [Change Management]. Heemstede, NL: Holland Business Publications, 1997.

META Group. "EAS Process Model: Evolution 2000." META Group, April 2000.

Nathans, H. *Adviseren als tweede beroep* [Consultancy as a Second Profession], 2nd ed. Deventer, NL: Kluwer, 1995.

Parker, M.M., and R. J. Benson. *Information Economics.* Englewood Cliffs, NJ: Prentice Hall, 1988.

Rosser, B. "IT Architecture by Time: Today, Tomorrow or Next Minute." Gartner Research Note, December 1999.

Sanden, W. van der, and B. Sturm. *Informatie-architectuur: De infrastructurele benadering* [Information Architecture: The Infrastructural Approach]. Rosmalen, NL: Panfox, 1997.

Schadler, T., S.D. Woodring, C.S. Overby, and J. Walker. "Getting Apps to Work Together." Forrester Research, June 1998.

Siegel, D. *Futurize your Enterprise: Business Strategy in the Age of the e-Customer.* New York: John Wiley & Sons, 1999.

Simons, J.L., and G.M.A. Verheijen. *Informatiestrategie als Management-opgave; Planning, Ontwikkeling en Beheer van Informatieverzorging op Basis van Information Engineering* [Information Strategy as Management issue: Planning, Development and Maintenance of Information Services on the Basis of Information Engineering]. Deventer, NL: Stenfert Kroese/Kluwer, 1991.

Stapleton, J. *DSDM™: De Methode in de Praktijk* [The Method in Practice]. Schoonhoven, NL: Academic Service, 1999.

Stroes, H.J., and M.E. Egberts. *Veranderen met Resultaat* [Changing with Results]. Deventer, NL: Kluwer, 1996.

Swede, V. Van. "Information Architecture: Relevance and Use as a Business—IT Alignment Tool." Cap Gemini Institute, 1999.

Thiadens, T. *Beheer van ICT-voorzieningen* [Management of IT Services], 3rd rev. ed. Schoonhoven, NL: Academic Service, 1999.

Torn, J.D. Van Der. "Management in Het Krachtenveld van de Organisatie." [Management in the Forcefield of the Organization]. *M&O: tijdschrift voor Organisatiekunde en Sociaal Beleid* 6 (1986): 482–501.

Treacy, M., and F.D. Wiersema. *The Discipline of Market Leaders: Choose Your Customers, Narrow Your Focus and Dominate Your Market.* London: Perseus, 1997.

Tuft, B. "Enterprise Architecture: Laying the e-Foundation for 21st-Century Business." Paper presented at Congress META Group, March 27–29, 2000, Munich.

Vaan, M.J.M. de, C.A.G. Sneep, A. Drukker, and S. ten Have. *Strategische Dialoog* [Strategic Dialog]. The Hague: Delwel Uitgeverij, 1998.

Wagter, R., and M. Kooij. *Informatiebeleid Volgens AIS* [Information Policy According to AIS]. Alphen aan den Rijn, NL: Samsom 1990.

Westbrock, T. "Architecture Process Maturity Revisited and Revised." META Group, May 2004.

Zachman, J.A. "Enterprise Architecture: The Issues of the Century." ZIFA, 1996.

Zee, H. van der, P. Laagland, B. Hafkenscheid, and L. Geersing (Nolan Norton Institute). *Architectuur als Managementinstrument: Multi Client Study* [Architecture as a Management Instrument: A Multiclient Study]. The Hague: Ten Hagen & Stam, 2000.

Ziadé, O. "eEnterprise Success in the New Millennium: The Role of Architecture." PTech, Inc., 2000.

INDEX

10 principles of DYA, 53

A
agility, 14, 21, 42, 88, 127, 153, 161, 195
allocation of architectural resources, 54
anticipatory strategy, 58, 61, 64, 67
application architecture, 106
application maintenance, 159
architect, 15, 28, 47, 53, 64, 81, 102, 120, 148, 158, 179, 183, 189
architectural domains, 39
architectural framework, 103
architectural principles, 107, 111,
architectural process, 179
Architectural Services, 60, 102, 189
architectural team, 44, 121, 158, 160, 178
architecture as a management tool, 41, 62, 183
architecture, 21, 37, 42
aspects of architecture, 42
auctioning model, 18

B
Balanced Score Card, 192
barrier, 45, 47, 67
behavior, 182
behavioral codes and values, 183
building permit, 149, 162
business architect, 124
business architecture, 39, 104
business case team, 81, 102, 157
business case, 60, 74, 111
business models, 18
business objectives, 74
business process, 15
business strategy, 18, 57

C
change process, 31, 41, 87
coherence, 14, 21, 88, 127, 161, 195